To: Gerald

Happy 70th Birthday,
11 July 2018

Love from
Diane &
Juliet
xx

A Sense of
OCCASION

Mendelssohn in 1846 from a painting by Eduard Magnus.
By kind permission of AKG London (The Arts and History Library).

A Sense of OCCASION

Mendelssohn in Birmingham 1846 & 1847

Audrey Duggan

BREWIN BOOKS

First published by
Brewin Books Ltd, 56 Alcester Road,
Studley, Warwickshire B80 7LG in 2011
www.brewinbooks.com

ISBN: 978-1-85858-449-2

A Cataloguing in Publication Record
for this title is available from the British Library.

Typeset in Baskerville
Printed in Great Britain by
Berforts Group Limited.

CONTENTS

ACKNOWLEDGEMENTS

I would like to thank AKG London (The Arts and History Picture Library) for their kind permission to use the photograph of Mendelssohn.
Much help has been gratefully received from staff in the Archives and Heritage Department at Birmingham Central Reference Library.

I would also like to thank my kind friends, Denis and Beryl McCready, for both reading the text and making a number of helpful suggestions.

I am much indebted to Professor George Caird, Principal of the Birmingham Conservatoire, University of Central England, for his generous provision of a Foreword at a time when he was already extremely busy.

Gordon Allen's foreword to this second edition is much appreciated, as is the help and advice both he and his wife, Margaret, have given.

I must also thank my friend and colleague, the late Jean Holland, whose help with proofreading has been invaluable.

I must not forget to thank Norman Ashfield, librarian at the Birmingham Conservatoire Library for his much needed assistance.

Finally, I owe considerable debt to Geoffrey, my husband, without whose encouragement and help with research, this book would not have been written.

PREFACE

After the bicentenary year of Mendelssohn's birth, it is fitting that there should be a revised and expanded re-issue of *A Sense of Occasion*, the story of *Elijah* in Birmingham.

Much has happened since the publication of the story in 1998. Then the future of Birmingham's Town Hall was precarious and it was feared in some quarters, that the city's greatest listed building might, even yet, be demolished.

Fortunately, these gloomy fears were not to be realized, and with the aid of English Heritage and lottery money, the magnificent building was recently restored. To celebrate this, a performance of Mendelssohn's *Elijah* was given on Sunday, 13 April, 2008. It was an event which attracted much interest, and was the first time that Mendelssohn's masterpiece was performed inside the newly refurbished building: an event for which I was asked to contribute an Introduction to the celebratory programme (reproduced here as Appendix 3).

The score used was, and now usually is, that of the revised version of *Elijah*; the one that the composer brought with him on his return to the city the following year. The story of that return is now told here for the first time. It is to be seen as completing the *Elijah* narrative and Birmingham's love affair with the composer. An oratorio that is woven irrevocably into the vivid tapestry that is the city's musical history.

Finally a word about method. To avoid unnecessary repetition, extracts from a single source but separated by brief commentary are referenced as one.

There is also the issue of language change. Today we talk of music festivals, but in 1873, J.T. Bunce in his authoritative History, uses the term 'musical festivals' as does the publicity of the day. I have opted for the modern version.

FOREWORD TO THE FIRST EDITION

Mendelssohn's visit to Birmingham in 1846 for the first performance of his oratorio, *Elijah* is one of the most celebrated events in the history of the City. Audrey Duggan has told the story of this visit with great clarity and in an extremely readable way. Her research has given us some fascinating details on Birmingham in the 1840's, on Mendelssohn's preparations for *Elijah* in London, on his journey to Birmingham and on his stay with Joseph Moore. Her account of the performance itself re-creates the atmosphere in the Town Hall splendidly. Descriptions of Mendelssohn himself as well as of the performers and the audience from newspaper reports give us a real glimpse of the personalities involved.

Audrey Duggan has also set this story in the wider context of the history of the Birmingham Festivals and how Mendelssohn came to be commissioned to write *Elijah*. This is a fascinating account and one which makes a valuable addition to the literature on Mendelssohn and on concert life in the middle of the 19th century.

George Caird, Principal of Birmingham Conservatoire, University of Central England.
October 1998

FOREWORD TO THE SECOND EDITION

It is always a delight to read a book about a subject you are familiar with that not only confirms what you already know but also fills in gaps in your knowledge. *A Sense of Occasion* is such a book.

In the first edition Audrey Duggan took us on a voyage of discovery telling us in her very personal style of the special relationship that developed between Mendelssohn and Birmingham. Now she takes us even further, bringing to light more details about Mendelssohn after the outstanding success of *Elijah* at the 1846 Triennial Birmingham Musical Festival in the crowded Town Hall.

The Festival Directors had established Birmingham Festival Choral Society in 1843 and stated that "the choruses, therefore, will be found more perfect and finished than they have ever been". This meant that there was a trained chorus in existence ready for the premiere of *Elijah* in 1846.

I am fortunate to be a singer with the present day BFCS which, on 13 April 2008, re-created that historic event by performing *Elijah* in the recently renovated Town Hall.

This is a factual tale told in an interesting, lively and informative way that will be appreciated not only by musicians but also by anyone who enjoys a well-told tale.

Gordon C. Allen: Archivist – Birmingham Festival Choral Society.

INTRODUCTION

This is not a history of Birmingham. Neither is it a biography of Mendelssohn or an analysis of his great oratorio, *Elijah*, as these topics have already been considered many times.

Instead it is an attempt to re-create for the general reader, a little of what is must have been like on and around the time of that fine day in August 1846, when Mendelssohn conducted the world premiere of his *Elijah* at the Birmingham Town Hall.

In the audience on that auspicious day were my great-great-grandfather, George, and his brother, Samuel. The fluctuating fortunes of the two men epitomise, with a clarity personal to me, the ease with which the aspiring middle-class could be both made and broken. For whereas Samuel, the successful businessman, lived in a mansion with a carriage and coach-house, George dwindled away a greater part of his life in inner-city Vincent Street. Finally, as the area became a slum, he was 'rescued' by his less than loving family to end his days ever-mindful of their charity…

It is a story that could be repeated many times throughout this period and is therefore neither remarkable nor unique. But in a small way it does illumine a strand of the social weave that was Birmingham in the 1840's: Mendelssohn's Birmingham and its people.

Chapter One

SETTING THE SCENE

We know something of what Mendelssohn thought about Birmingham from a swiftly executed pen and ink sketch that he made. It depicts a passenger train, a multitude of factory chimneys belching black smoke, an advertisement for Warren's Blacking and numerous workshops crowding around the Town Hall. This is framed within the arch of a huge viaduct. All that is missing are the church spires: those of St Phillip's, St Martin's, Christchurch and St Paul's.

At a glance we are given a bird's eye view: a stroke of the pen and materialised are the reasons for Birmingham's prosperity; industry and trade

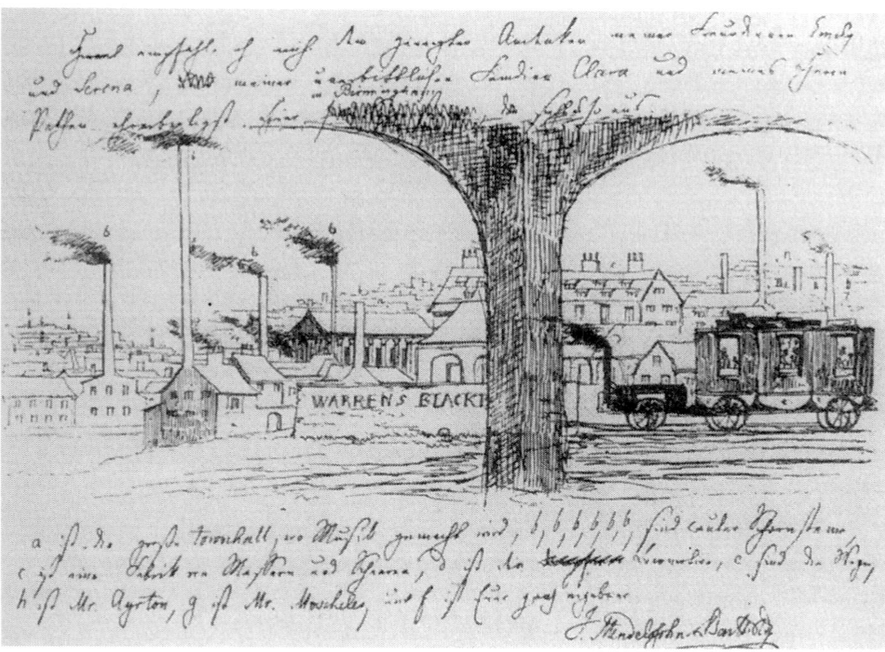

Birmingham. From a pen drawing by Mendelssohn.

and the ugly dereliction that frequently followed in their wake. A Yorkshire proverb sums it up: "Where there's muck there's brass!" But to return to the churches. Had they been in this sketch, they would have provided a more complete picture: a glimmer of something other, a differing aspiration. For in 1846, Birmingham also had much to be proud of. It had its General Hospital and its renowned Music Festivals which are the lynch-pin of this account. It had its new Market Hall with those tremendous columns: its Town Hall, its Curzon Street passenger and goods stations.

But most importantly for the events that are to be described, Birmingham now had a revitalised New Street. New Street had recently been macadamised. It had raised paving and gas street-lighting and new shops. Here was Christchurch towering at its apex with Colmore Row. Here the Society of Arts, had recently opened its doors and was housed in a building described by local historian, William Hutton, as:

> a chaste and elegant specimen of the Corinthian order, with a boldly projecting portico of four elegant columns ...

Hutton is proud of its inception; it was, he says:

> instituted in 1821 for promoting the general study of the fine arts by procuring from the nobility and gentry who are its patrons, the loan of original pictures of the ancient and modern schools, in order to stimulate the genius and industry of its members ...[1]

Further along the New Royal Hotel, a conversion of Beau Green's Portugal House, was now open for business. On this site was later to stand the new Pinfold Street Post Office. However, in Mendelssohn's day, the Bennetts Hill office was still functioning with what Hutton describes as a newly added "piazza" so that "the public could transact their business" without getting wet. On the site of what is now Café Rouge and other outlets was the Theatre Royal.

At the top of New Street stood the Town Hall. Built originally as a Music Hall to rival facilities provided in other parts of the country for concert going, its architect was Joseph Hansom of Hansom Cab fame. The building was intended to replicate the Temple of Jupiter Stater in Rome and among its many classical features were thirty-two Corinthian columns each thirty-six feet high and three-foot-six in diameter. Built of brick and faced with Anglesey Marble, it was considered by the city fathers to be a suitable setting for the staging of what had become Birmingham's widely renowned Music Festivals.

It was a building appreciated in a description of poetic beauty by Charles Reece Pemberton:

Town Hall & Christchurch (1840's).

> The Birmingham Town Hall is a noble edifice – look at it from any of the five lines of approach – you will. Seen under a very clear sky, it is silent glory and beauty; under the night light of the moon is now *dark'd,* now flashed out again suddenly, by the rapidly-scudding black storm clouds, it is, of all the buildings I remember in the kingdom, the most thought-suggestive.[2]

Unfortunately, no description of the Town Hall at this time is complete without mention of the slum properties that can be seen in old wood-cuts

Curzon Street Station in 1846.

New Street in the 1840's showing the Society of Arts building.

crowding up the Hill Street of the day. A Birmingham Quaker, William White, describes how things were:

> From Worcester Street and Smallbrook Street up to the Town Hall and crowding the hill closely behind New Street, these discreditable slums existed under the names of the Old Inkleys, the New Inkleys, Tonk Street, Peek Lane, the Froggary, King, Queen and Pinfold Street ... and our noble Town Hall itself was hemmed in on three sides by buildings in a similar condition.[3]

It is a view not held by Reece Pemberton. He approves of the fact that the Town Hall stands near to "humble brick dwelling-houses". He sees it as their "magnificent friend" and continues:

> Had its site been more elevated ground and its whole more isolated, I think it would not have possessed that look of the kindly grand, that countenance of the benevolently beautiful, which ... it now possesses.

So there we have it: two men of widely differing views: the one a reformer, the other a poet, both contributing in their own way to a picture of Birmingham in the 1840's.

However, for *us* to imagine what life was really like with its market traders, horse-drawn vehicles, extremes of wealth and poverty, requires an imaginative leap of almost epic proportions. The Industrial Revolution was on its way, Birmingham was fast becoming 'the toy-shop of Europe': but even so I can't help feeling that life in the middle of the nineteenth century had still more in common with the past than the future.

One thing we can be sure of. On that Wednesday in August 1846, the crowds gathering along the length of New Street to watch the procession of 'elegant equipages' as their occupants drove to the Town Hall to hear the world premiere of *Elijah*, would have closed their eyes to the slums behind and firmly fixed their gaze to the front.

Old view of the Town Hall, from Hill Street. From an original drawing.

Chapter Two

BEFORE THE CONCERT

Mendelssohn's visit had been widely publicised, his *Elijah* receiving considerable coverage in *The Times* of the previous Monday, 24 August. Here a detailed description of the oratorio gave readers an account of what they could expect: "the awful prediction of Elijah the Tishbite provoked by the iniquities of Ahab": an idea represented in the opening bass recitative.

This spread of nearly two thousand words, illustrated the enormous interest engendered by the work. Of course the story of Elijah from the *Old Testament's First Book of Kings* would have helped. Its theme, that of confrontation between good and evil as represented by Elijah, Jehovah's representative, and Baal the pagan god of the "unbeliever" and his follower King Ahab, would have been well-known to Victorian church-going audiences: and it was dramatic enough to whet even the tardiest appetite.

The composer had visited Birmingham's Festivals on two previous occasions, had charmed with his delightful manners, and been charmed in return. On an earlier occasion[1] he had thrilled his audience by extemporising on the organ; then his oratorio *St. Paul* had been widely acclaimed. Now, poised between anticipation and reality, his Birmingham admirers were not going to let him down.

It was a grand social occasion. Everybody who was anybody was there and for many it was gratifying that their names on the Guest List of the Festival Committee, were duly reported in the press.

The press whipped up the general excitement. It told of the vast crowds that thronged the whole of New Street on that day, from the Hen and Chickens Hotel at the Bull Ring end right up to the doors of the Town Hall at the top.

> We said the streets were crowded yesterday: today they were damned up; there was no road for foot passengers; the whole length of New Street, from the Hen and Chickens to the Music Hall was lined on each

DEPARTURE & ARRIVAL OF RAILWAY TRAINS.
LONDON & NORTH-WESTERN RAILWAY.
(Southern Division.)

FROM BIRMINGHAM TO LONDON.

DEPARTURE.		ARRIVAL.
From Birmingham.		*At London.*
12 55 A.M.	Mail, mixed	5 18 A.M.
7 0 A.M.	Mixed, fast	11 25 A.M.
7 45 A.M.	Mixed	12 35 P.M.
9 30 A.M.	Mail, First Class	1 0 P.M.
10 10 A.M.	Mixed	2 45 P.M.
12 0 noon.	Mixed	5 0 P.M.
12 35 P.M.	Third Class	7 0 P.M.
1 30 P.M.	Mixed, Fast	6 0 P.M.
4 0 P.M.	Mixed	8 45 P.M.
5 45 P.M.	Mixed	10 15 P.M.
7 50 P.M.	Express, First Class only	11 0 P.M.
From Rugby.		
1 15 a.m.	Mail Mixed	4 45 a.m.
6 50 a.m.	Mixed	10 10 a.m.
12 45 p.m.	Mixed	4 0 p.m.
4 15 p.m.	Mixed	7 30 p.m.
5 0 p.m.	Mixed	7 55 p.m.
6 45 p.m.	Express, First Class only	9 10 p.m.

From Blisworth. To London.	*From Wolverton.*
12 57 p.m. Mixed... 3 20 p.m.	6 45 a.m. Mixed... 9 15 a.m.
6 0 p.m. Mixed... 8 30 p.m.	*From Bletchley.*
From Aylesbury.	10 20 a.m. Mixed... 12 0 noon.
7 0 a.m. Mixed... 9 15 a.m.	*From Watford.*
10 45 a.m. Mixed... 12 30 p.m.	9 0 a.m. .... 10 0 a.m.
2 45 p.m. Mixed... 4 15 p.m.	*From Birmingham to Rugby.*
6 45 p.m. Mixed... 9 35 p.m.	8 15 p.m. Mixed... 9 30 p.m.

FROM LONDON TO BIRMINGHAM.

DEPARTURE.		ARRIVAL.
From London.		*At Birmingham.*
6 15 a.m.	Mixed	10 50 a.m.
7 0 a.m.	Third Class	2 40 p.m.
7 30 a.m.	Mixed	12 55 p.m.
8 30 a.m.	Mixed	12 45 p.m.
10 0 a.m.	Mail, First Class only	1 25 p.m.
11 0 a.m.	Mixed	3 35 p.m.
12 30 p.m.	Mixed	5 35 p.m.
2 45 p.m.	Mixed	7 15 p.m.
5 0 p.m.	Express, First Class only	8 0 p.m.
5 30 p.m.	Mixed	10 0 p.m.
8 45 p.m.	Mail, Mixed	1 5 a.m.
		At Rugby.
9 0 a.m.	Mixed	11 55 a.m.
9 25 a.m.	Express, First Class only	11 40 a.m.
10 30 a.m.	Mixed	1 30 p.m.
12 0 noon,	Mixed	3 15 p.m.
4 0 p.m.	Mixed	6 45 p.m.
9 0 p.m.	Mail, Mixed	12 0 p.m.

To Watford.	*From London. To Tring.*
10 0 p.m. Mixed...10 45 p.m.	5 5 p.m. Mixed.....6 30 p.m.
To Aylesbury.	*To Bletchley.*
11 10 a.m. Mixed ... 1 0 p.m.	3 45 p.m. Mixed... 5 18 p.m.
3 0 p.m. Mixed ... 4 45 p.m.	*To Wolverton.*
To Blisworth.	6 0 p.m. Mixed ....8 20 p.m.
10 45 a.m. Mixed ...12 55 p.m.	*From Rugby to Birmingham.*
	8 0 a.m. Mixed.....9 35 a.m.

ON SUNDAYS.

From Birmingham.		*Arrival in London.*
12 55 a.m.	Mail, mixed	5 18 a.m.
9 30 a.m.	Mail, first class only	1 30 p.m.
12 35 p.m.	Third class	7 20 p.m.
1 30 p.m.	Mixed	6 45 p.m.
From Rugby.		
1 15 a.m.	Mail, mixed	4 45 a.m.

From Aylesbury. To London.	*From Wolverton*
7 0 a.m. Mixed ... 9 15 a.m.	6 45 a.m. Mixed... 9 15 a.m.
7 0 p.m. Mixed ... 9 0 p.m.	

From London.		*Arrival in Birmingham.*
7 0 a.m.	Third Class	2 40 p.m.
7 30 a.m.	Mixed	12 35 p.m.
10 0 a.m.	Mail, First Class	1 25 p.m.
8 45 p.m.	Mail, mixed	1 5 a.m.
		To Rugby.
9 0 p.m.	Mail, mixed	12 0 p.m.

To Aylesbury.	*From London. To Wolverton.*
8 30 a.m. Mixed ...10 30 a.m.	6 0 p.m. Mixed .. 8 20 p.m.

BIRMINGHAM AND WARWICK AND LEAMINGTON.

From Birmingm. to Leamington.	*From Leamington to Birmingm.*
7 45 a.m. .... 9 0 a.m.	7 50 a.m. .... 9 35 a.m.
9 30 a.m. .... 10 35 a.m.	9 25 a.m. .... 10 50 a.m.
10 10 a.m. .... 11 25 a.m.	10 15 a.m. .... 12 35 p.m.
12 0 noon......... 1 15 p.m.	12 10 p.m......... 1 25 p.m.
1 30 p.m. .... 3 20 p.m.	2 10 p.m. .... 3 35 p.m.
4 0 p.m. .... 5 15 p.m.	4 5 p.m. .... 5 35 p.m.
5 45 p.m. .... 7 10 p.m.	5 50 p.m. .... 7 15 p.m.
8 15 p.m. .... 9 45 p.m.	6 50 p.m. .... 8 0 p.m.
From Coventry to Leamington.	8 35 p.m. .... 10 0 p.m.

Train timetable.

> side with a dense mass of human beings, eager to behold the visitors as they made their way to the building.[2]

and later:

> the tops of the houses, and every window from garret to ground floor, were covered and crowded with spectators.

All the signs were auspicious. Earlier in the week, the weather, as it often is, had been unpredictable but on this Wednesday it relented. The press made much of it.

> the sun, moreover, in one of its best moods, shone brightly upon the animated scene and lent it a glory not its own.

On the road at this time were a bewildering number of horse-drawn vehicles. There was the landau, with its two pram-like hoods that could be raised or lowered, one at each end of the carriage. These were used chiefly for riding in the park. There were phaetons, victorias, curricles, cabriolets and dog-carts to name but a few more. However, in a contemporary picture[3] of people arriving in Birmingham for the concert, it is the brougham (pronounced broom) that is the most popular. It is from the brougham that visitors can be seen stepping down at the doors of the Town Hall, whilst others arriving on foot are directed to another side entrance.

The latter were popular because they were adaptable. They were favoured by the aristocracy, but less expensive models were within the pocket of the middle-class, many of whom would have wished to emulate their 'betters'.

From pictures, it can be seen that the brougham was a four-wheeled horse-drawn cab. A top-of-the-range model would have had sprung seating for four to six people. A party of them would have sat, as we do today in a taxi, facing each other. It would have been designed with a circular front instead of the more usual square and it would have been pulled by a pair of horses.

However, most of the pictures of the day record a monopoly of one-horse broughams: but one horse or not, up front and outside each vehicle would have sat the coachman in his livery.

Up New Street on 26 August 1846, rolled these "elegant equipages".[4] A procession of well-groomed horses: greys, bays and blacks pulling carriages of different size and design. The doors of the cabs would have been polished to a mirror and borne, if the occupant were an aristocrat or even a member of the minor gentry, his coat of arms emblazoned upon them.

The coachman, too, would have provided a focus of interest: each with his livery designed to show to advantage the status and social standing of the family who employed him.

For many hours, because people began to arrive early, the street would have been filled with carriages. Their presence on that Wednesday morning was what the people had come to see. They had staked a claim, rather as visitors today might do for the State Opening of Parliament, and they would not have been disappointed.

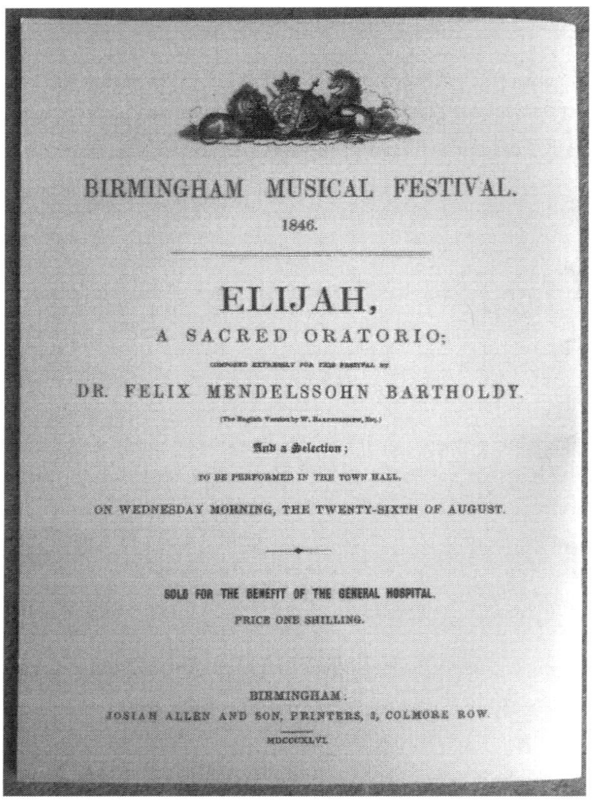
BIRMINGHAM MUSICAL FESTIVAL.

1846.

ELIJAH,

A SACRED ORATORIO;

DR. FELIX MENDELSSOHN BARTHOLDY.

And a Selection;

TO BE PERFORMED IN THE TOWN HALL,

ON WEDNESDAY MORNING, THE TWENTY-SIXTH OF AUGUST.

SOLD FOR THE BENEFIT OF THE GENERAL HOSPITAL.

PRICE ONE SHILLING.

BIRMINGHAM:

JOSIAH ALLEN AND SON, PRINTERS, 3, COLMORE ROW.

MDCCCXLVI.

Front cover of programme, 26 August 1846.

Chapter Three

THE CONCERT

People attending the concert would have read about travel and ticket arrangements in *Aris's Gazette*, a weekly broad-sheet which in an age of no radio or television, provided an important means of communication. Directions for those travelling by brougham to the Town Hall were explicit. No infringement of the rules, which applied both to those arriving at and those leaving the building, would be tolerated. For those with reserved seats:

> Carriages will set down and take up in a single line, as will those taking Company to or from the Galleries and the Secured seats on the floor of the Hall. They will come up the North Side of New Street and through the barrier on the same side setting down with their horses' heads towards the Navigation Office, in Paradise Street and drawing off along Paradise Street, or turning down the South Side of New Street.[1] (sic)

If on the other hand you had an unsecured seat or were standing, you were instructed:

> (to) come along the West side of Ann-Street (modern Colmore Row) and through the barrier on the same side, with (your) Horses' heads towards Congreve Street ... (sic)

In order to avoid congestion, the time a carriage was permitted to stop was regulated; "No carriage can be allowed to stand more than two minutes at the doors." Should an infringement occur the coachman would be required by the police to move on and take his place at the back of the queue.

> The regulations will be strictly enforced by the police and gentlemen are earnestly requested to order their coachmen to comply therewith.

For the week of the Festival, tickets were obtainable from the ticket-office and only the ticket-office at 24 Waterloo Street. Doors were open from eight a.m. until one in the afternoon and from two until nine in the evening. The price of a secured seat was one pound, "other places" were ten shillings and sixpence: gentlemen were reminded not to send their servants into the Hall to reserve seats, a device to which the authorities had grown wise over the years.

In spite of all this, well over two thousand people were to plough their way through the intricacies of officialdom, eventually to find themselves in a magnificent Hall where the excitement outside was more than matched by the excitement within.

The Town Hall had recently been newly decorated and refurbished "under the direction of Mr Crace of London" a rather grand way of describing the services of what we, today, might call an interior designer. The *London Illustrated News* is agreeably impressed:

> The blending of the colours is charming. The ceiling is divided into three large circles and studded with rosettes and panels, painted blue and white on a cream and chocolate ground alternatively ... the seats have been painted a dark mahogany with red cushions.[2]

Seating is worth a comment. In fact the arrangements, by our standards, were far from adequate. The audience sat on benches and in spite of the much acclaimed new cushions, was packed in very closely. Seats, except those for illustrious guests, were unreserved. Even the London press was not catered for.

> The first view of the Hall as we entered the great gallery to find *what standing place we could* was altogether dazzling. Every nook and corner was alive, not a vacant spot was to be seen.[3]

Not only was the press left to stand. A number of the audience stood throughout the performance too. Fire regulations at this time were non-existent and as people were permitted to bring their own folding stools and 'camp' in the aisles, the fire-risk would have been considerable.

Figures vary enormously as to how many people the Town Hall could hold; but a reasonable estimate would be that there were upwards of two

Waterloo Street and Christchurch 1898. Photograph by Thomas Clarke.

and a half thousand in the audience on that day. So a crisis would have induced a stampede.

Once everyone was seated, the eyes of all would have been directed towards the platform. For there, and forming a riveting centre-piece, rose the great organ.

The Times rhapsodises:

> The immense organ with its thirty-two feet pipes, looking like gigantic rolls of oil-cloth, rose up from behind till its head touched the roof, like some vast animal of mysterious form.

The London Illustrated News adds:

> The organ-case has been splendidly embellished and the pipes gilt with gold scrolls ...

As an after-thought and rather inconsequentially it continues:

> ... a judicious sprinkling of arabesques add to the beauty of the ceiling.

It is not surprising that the great organ came in for considerable comment, for it was (and is) most impressive. Built by William Hill in 1832, it has a wooden case which is forty feet high, forty feet wide and seventeen feet deep. Its largest metal pipe standing in front of this case is thirty-five feet three inches long and five feet four and a half inches in circumference. Newly decorated, it would have dominated even the largest of rooms; and this is before we begin to consider the glorious sound that it made.

The press, too, has an eye for the ladies who merit some rather heavy-handed flattery. *The Times*:

> The beautiful toilettes of the ladies harmonised exquisitely with the new decoration of the Hall ...

and not to be outdone, *The Birmingham Gazette* describes the 'gaiety' and 'bloom' that their presence brought to the proceedings.

A word about fashion would not be out of place here. At this time, most of the well-dressed men in the audience would have been wearing either a tail or a frock-coat. The tail-coat, as the name implies, was worn fastened and fitted at the waist in front but with two square tails that hung down at the back. The frock-coat, on the other hand, would have been worn unbuttoned, was not cut away at the front and would have reached down all round to about the knees. All the men would have worn top-hats and light summer boots, and carried both gloves and a cane. A waistcoat made

The Grand Organ in the Town Hall, Birmingham.

of eye-catching silk, patterned with stripes or dots would have completed the effect and produced a flash of colour in an otherwise sombre outfit.

It would have been left to the ladies to provide more colour. In 1846 lilac was exceedingly popular, but pinks, blues and creams would also have been much in evidence. The ladies, too, would have dressed for the occasion, and as this was the age of the tightly laced corset – an eighteen-inch waist was much admired – their dresses were designed to draw attention to this.

The effect was achieved in a number of ways. Skirts were voluminous and worn, depending upon the time of year, over 4-7 petticoats, one of which would have been stiffened with horse-hair. These would have contrasted with a tightly-fitting bodice so drawing attention to a tiny waist. The bodice itself, with its décolleté neckline, its tight, short and braided sleeves emerging from a wide dropped shoulder line, would also serve to display to advantage a slim waist which could comfortably have been spanned by the fingers of each hand.

Ladies, too, wore light boots and from contemporary paintings it can be seen that they also wore russes (pieces of styled lace) in their hair. Hair must have caused some problems, at least for the maid. It was styled principally in side-curls or ringlets, an effect achieved by means of curl-papers and tongs. All the ladies would have carried fans and on that August day with the sun streaming through the window, they would have needed them. For their tightly laced corsets would have been hot and so would their numerous petticoats.

They would have been uncomfortable, too, in other ways. As is shown on the *Town Hall Plans and Written Specification for 1848*, the original ONE water-closet in the ladies' cloak-room was to be renewed. One water-closet for the use of hundreds of women[4] over a period of up to four hours (for a number would have arrived early) was a situation upon which it is better not to dwell!

Of many of the people packed so tightly into this audience there is no record. But the same is not true of those who were subscribers. A glance at the attendance list in *The Times* will confirm that such people were prioritised according to rank. First came the aristocracy, then high-ranking churchmen followed by representatives of the armed forces. After these came the lower orders of clergy and the middle classes. This was an age when people knew their place! Many had come a fair distance and would have been staying at the town's well-known hostelries: such as Dee's Royal Hotel where Wrottesley, the President, spent the week, or the Stork Hotel in the Old Square (today that would be near to the site of Temple Court, Ministry of Justice), or the Hen and Chickens in New Street.

Finding out about some of these people is a fascinating experience. Take for example Captain John Forrest of the Eleventh Hussars. At this time he was a young man at the beginning of what was going to prove a most successful career. Would he then have guessed that years later he was to serve in the Crimean Campaign? Be wounded at Balaclava and present at Inkerman? Of course not: but he did and was.

At the time of the concert, Forrest was involved in a controversy with Lord Cardigan of *Charge of the Light Brigade* fame or notoriety. The former requested an extension of compassionate leave to be with his wife who was ill after the birth of their first child. The latter had no compunction in refusing. Upon being appealed to, the Duke of Wellington, to his credit, sided with the young officer, and was moved to comment that if his army could not be commanded without such "voluminous correspondence and such futile details", he would need to employ extra staff. Forrest was to end his career as a general and collect many honours along the way.

Then, more importantly, there is the President of the Birmingham Festival. Trained as a lawyer, Lord Wrottesley, Second Baron Wrottesley, of

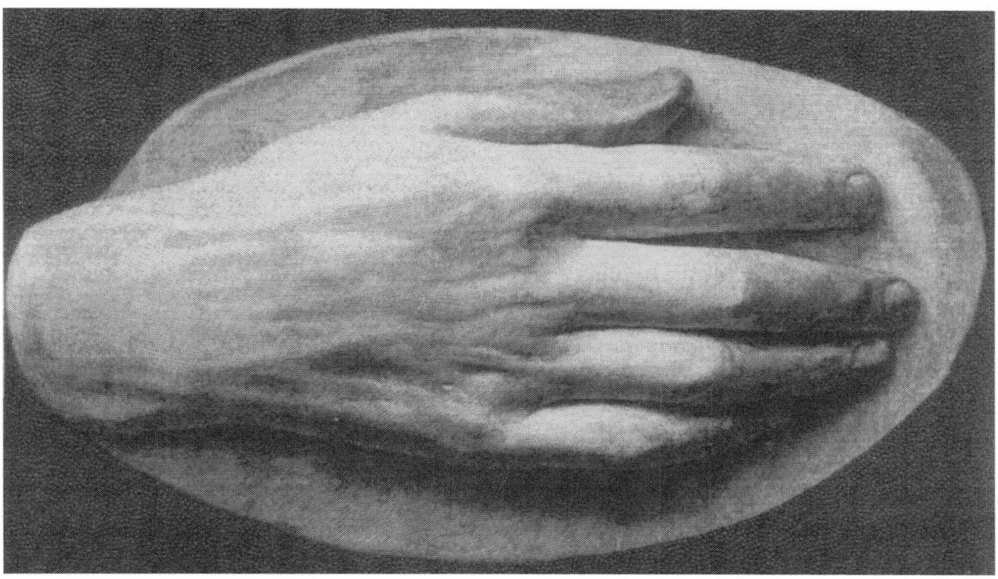

Mendelssohn's hand.

Wrottesley Hall, now the club-house of Tettenhall Golf Club in Staffordshire, is interesting because of his abiding passion which was astronomy. For Wrottesley was the 'Patrick Moore' of his day. He, too, had an observatory built in his grounds, and the fruit of his labours was, *A Catalogue of the Right Ascension of 1318 Stars*. With others he was responsible for the founding of the Royal Astronomical Society, and after being elected a fellow was ultimately to become its president.

Wrottesley was a wealthy man but he was also generous. Upon leaving the Mendelssohn concert he donated a hundred pounds towards the General Hospital, worth around five thousand pounds today.

Lord Wrottesley took his duties as President of the Festival seriously. He attended every concert and the Gala Ball with which the festivities ended although, unfortunately, the dance music played then came in for much criticism (see chapter 6).

Next there is the Countess Haan-Haan listed as "that celebrated Eastern traveller". "Celebrated" she certainly was but not so much for travelling as the beds she slept in and with whom. Married at an early age to her cousin, hence the hyphenated name, the unsatisfactory marriage was soon annulled. The unfortunate experience however, fired her creative abilities and she launched into a series of novels about romantically dissatisfied young women. One does not need to be a psychiatrist to have something to say about that. In 1850 she became a Roman Catholic, and the convent she founded at Mainz was to be her home until her death. Now those romantic themes gave way to ones of a religious flavour which were to increase in fervour as her life neared its end; perhaps a very human turn of events.

Then there is the local Birmingham M.P., George Frederick Muntz. Muntz was nothing if not a character. James Grant, a colleague, has left an amusing description of the man who was, by all accounts, a remarkable individual.

> I have seen many well-whiskered faces ... but in the article of size, Mr Muntz's beard and whiskers throw all the other beards and whiskers I have seen completely into the shade.[5]

His face, Mr Grant continues, "is covered with one dense mass of long, black hair."

From Muntz we get Muntz Metal[6], a product that helped to make him rich. Also Muntz Street in the centre of Birmingham by which we can remember him. For Muntz is a man worth remembering. He held liberal views, advocated democratic reform and Catholic Emancipation. He was active in local politics and steadfastly opposed church rates. On one occasion this landed him in trouble. He appeared at Warwick Crown Court before Mr Justice Park on a charge, subsequently thrown out, of riotous assembly after having demanded and been refused to see St Martin's Church 'books' accounts.

He was a popular public speaker, but of his abilities as a parliamentarian Grant speaks more cautiously. He was not, he tells us,

> noted for the regularity of his attendance in his place at parliament – makes a point of 'looking in' as he calls it, every evening ...

Grant is also moved to a description of this gentleman's trousers. They were, "...of unprecedented thickness, of a dark colour and rough and woolly aspect." Apparently they were extremely wide, wider than sailors' trousers; but what really amuses the writer is not just "the singularity of the garment" but the fact that he wore them all the year round!

At a concert we are able to visualise Muntz very clearly because of the way that he used to sit. He would place "his hands on top of his stick and then rest his head on his hands." Muntz was a colourful character; a little larger than life, one that might have stepped straight out of Dickens.

Also in the audience on that morning was Sir William Sterndale Bennett, the English composer and friend of Mendelssohn. The two had first met at a concert in London in 1833. The former was then a student and had been playing his own *Concerto in D Minor* at the Royal Academy of Music, London, where he was studying. Mendelssohn was in the audience and it was his enthusiastic reception of the piece that encouraged the then young William to visit Leipzig for a year to be near the composer and to learn from him.

A decade later Mendelssohn's 'Christmas Gift', a testament supporting Sterndale Bennett in his application for the post of Professor of Music at Edinburgh University in 1843, shows how highly he thought of the Englishman's work. Referring to Sterndale Bennett's stay in Germany he writes:

> Your Overtures, your Concertos, your vocal as well as instrumental compositions, are reckoned ... amongst the first standard works of the present musical period.[7]

He continues by pointing out that the composer has been instrumental in destroying the 'prejudice' that English music at the time had been subject to: "... and so by your successes here you destroyed that prejudice which nobody but a true Genius (could have done)."

Such appreciation of the Englishman's gifts is seconded by Grove:

> When it is again recognised that musical composition is ... not a mere method of jumbling sounds together ... it is probable that Bennett will receive much higher credit than has yet been accorded to him ...[8]

There are some who may find that this concept of composition as "a mere method of jumbling sounds together" has resonances for today and it would seem to be true that Bennett's work, did not and never has met with the acclaim it might well have deserved.

But now let Mendelssohn's friend, Sir Julius Benedict, take up the story.

> The noble Town Hall was crowded ... with a brilliant and eagerly expectant audience. It was an anxious and solemn moment ... every eye had long been directed towards the conductor's desk ...[9]

By now the chorus and orchestra were in place. The choir was two-hundred and seventy-one strong. It was made up of seventy-nine sopranos, sixty male altos, "bearded altos" as Mendelssohn called them, sixty tenors and seventy-two basses. Among these on that day was William Pountney, a Birmingham chorister whose *Memoirs* of the rehearsal and the occasion, itself, are invaluable.

Much of the chorus was local; only sixty-two singers came from London. The opposite, however, was true of the orchestra which was primarily London-based. Mendelssohn's band as it was then called, was comprised broadly of an amalgamation of two London orchestras; the *London Opera* and members of the *Philharmonic Society Orchestra*. Even so, there was quite a sprinkling of local talent. A glance at the programme tells us that a number of violinists were local including: Flersheim, Allwood, Start, Beere, Hayward, Hawkes, Timmins and Jones. Four of the violas were Birmingham men: Wood, Grady, Heath and Adderley. Of the rest of the instruments; two 'cellos came from Birmingham and, likewise, two double-basses, two flutes, oboes and clarinets. One of the trumpets was a local man as was one of the ophicleides. That just leaves the drums, also played by a local musician, with the double drums coming from London.

Apparently, among this local talent was a thirteen-year old boy, Edward Bache from Edgbaston. His name does not appear on the programme so he must have been allowed to take part 'unofficially'. That he did play is vouched for by a number of friends and family. The boy's mother writes to her nephew, Russell Martineau, about the occasion:

> And where was your cousin all the time? He was in the orchestra very near his old master Mr (Alfred) Mellon and our kind friend Mr Flersheim, and thus had the great advantage ... of ... taking his part on the violin; it has been a great stimulus to him and encouragement.[10]

Mellon and Flersheim's names do appear on the programme and with the others would have been part of a country-wide network of talented amateur musicians who supplemented the professionals. Work was obtained by means of an introduction to the secretary of the requisite Festival; men like Joseph Moore who dominated the Birmingham scene for over half a century.

The following letter from Thos. Fletcher, who played at an earlier Festival, to the Liverpool solicitor, J.D. Grimshaw a talented amateur double-bass player, shows how the system worked.

> Bull St.
> 5.2.34.
>
> Dear Sir
>
> I have arranged with Mr Moore, the Manager of the ensuing Festival, for you to appear as a double base (sic) performer of which you shall have more particulars ...
>
> Yours
> Most Truly
> Thos. Fletcher.[11]

Mendelssohn's band comprised a hundred and twenty-five players; a number that by the standards of the day was large. Of these, ninety-three were string players. There were three flautists, four oboeists, four clarinettists, and four horn-players. The remainder of the players were made up of: four bassoonists, four trumpets, three ophicleides, and two drums.

The orchestra was different in a number of ways from what we might expect today. Today, for example, the ophicleide is no longer (or very rarely) used. This is because the invention of the bass-tuba in the 1880's rendered it obsolete.

Belonging to the keyed bugle family, the ophicleide was used in the nineteenth century to play parts which today are performed on the tuba. In military bands it was the chief bass instrument and very popular. Mendelssohn particularly specified three ophicleides and these he had placed at the back of the band. One of them, as can be seen from the programme (see page 96), was a monstre (sic) ophicleide, which, with its enormous trumpet-like looped brass body, played in an upright position, would have looked especially imposing. Next to these were the trombones and trumpets. Parallel and placed on either side of the brass were the great drums from the Tower.

The Times mentions these 'Tower drums' which got their name from the fact that they were at one time kept in the Tower of London. An original pair were alleged to have been plundered by Marlborough at the battle of Malplaquet but the ones used by Mendelssohn are likely to have been larger, measuring 39-inches and 35-inches in diameter. These were given the same name because of a story which alleged that the drum-head of one of them was made from the skin of a lion once kept at the Tower Zoo. Today these kettle drums are known as timpani and would be of varying sizes and numbers to suit the occasion.

The choir, ranged in front of the orchestra (today it would be massed at the back) was divided as follows. On the left were the sopranos and immediately behind them the tenors. On the opposite side were the altos and standing behind them the basses. *The Times* likes it:

> This arrangement, while it adds to the powers of the chorus also gives extreme sweetness to the effect, in consequence of the female voices being so near the front.[12]

Not much misses the eye of the press. Even the conductor's 'chair', a concession to those then not very distant days, when orchestras were directed from the piano or the first desk of the violins, comes in for comment. In Mendelssohn's case this took the form of a covered velvet stool. *The Times* describes it:

> The chair which is covered with Utrecht velvet is placed on a pedestal and is encircled with a light brass rail. It is very elegant and chaste.

When Mendelssohn stepped out on to the rostrum he was greeted with thunderous applause; not only by the audience but by the orchestra and chorus as well. Sir Julius Benedict, an English composer, conductor and personal friend, was among the audience and describes the moment:

> ... at half-past eleven o'clock a deafening shout from the band and chorus announced the approach of the great composer. The reception he met with was absolutely overwhelming; whilst the sun, emerging at that moment, seemed to illumine the vast edifice in honour of the bright and pure being who stood there the idol of all beholders.[13]

Even accounting for the hyperbole of the piece which is representative of the 'flowery' style of the time, it must have been a long awaited (many in the audience had been in their places for hours) and exhilarating moment. *The Times* agrees:

> The forms of etiquette were unanimously laid aside and one loud and universal cheer acknowledged the presence of the greatest composer of the age.

* * * * *

With the arrival of Mendelssohn, but before the concert gets under way, it is time for a brief digression. What was it about this man that made him so popular with colleagues and audiences alike? For often, although great men (and women) are revered by their public, they are not always easy to work with and frequently not especially likeable. That Mendelssohn was likeable is well attested. He had a great sense of humour as well as a prodigious capacity for work: and laughter is often a better task-master than admonishment.

The composer's humour is well illustrated by a delightful story concerning the oboeist, Grattan Cooke. Cooke had played under Mendelssohn on numerous occasions and the two were firm friends. Indeed, it has been suggested that the oboe obligato in *Elijah*, '*For The Mountains Shall Depart*', was especially written for him. This is by no means certain, but it is true that when the local score was first published, Mendelssohn presented the player with an inscribed copy of the score. Inside he had written the following:

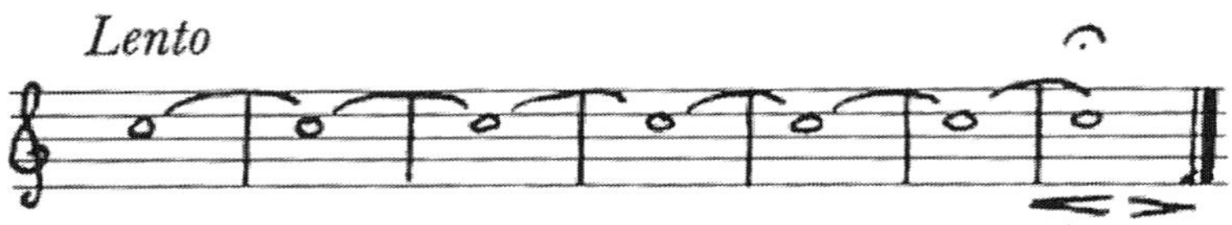

An Grattan Cooke, zum freundlichen Andenken.
Felix Mendelssohn-Bartholdy. London, Frühling, 1847.
(To Gratton Cooke with fond memories)
London, Spring, 1847.[14]

Of course what is required is an impossibility! As one can see, the same note is to be held for seven bars at a slow tempo. Not only is the last bar prolonged indefinitely, but the performer is required to execute both a crescendo and a decrescendo. No oboeist would be able to hold a single note for such a length of time and in the final bar still have enough breath to produce what is required. A contemporary musician puts it like this:

> Any oboeist who would dare to try and sustain that (last) note as directed would before bringing it to a termination, himself cease to exist![15]

Mendelssohn's 'joke' is likely to have been in response to an earlier one played on him by Cooke. This happened years before, at the start of a rehearsal for *A Midsummer Night's Dream* overture in London in 1831. Cooke, always punctual, was not in his seat, but soon to be seen on his way in to the room carrying a ladder! The inevitable questioning which presumably was the object of the whole exercise, resulted in the following reply:

> He's written the notes so tremendously high, that I've brought a ladder to get up to them.[16]

The same good humour was apparent in Birmingham in 1846. *The Birmingham Journal*, present at the full rehearsal of *A Midsummer Night's Dream* overture in the Town Hall on the previous Monday morning, describes what went on:

> … a rattle of his baton on the music stand brings the band to a dead halt. 'Gentlemen' says Mendelssohn, 'that won't do. All FORTISSIMO, all PIANISSIMO, no PIANO. A little PIANO between if you please. Must have PIANO, gentlemen; when you come to FORTISSIMO, do as you like'.[17]

But the paper continues:

> All is expressed with animation and good humour, and a roar of laughter over, the band tries again, and a smile playing on the expressive features of the conductor, attests the power of his pleasantly administered corrective.

To both animation and good humour may be added Mendelssohn's courtesy. Part of his reply to Joseph Moore's invitation to come to Birmingham in 1846 illustrates this.

> Frankfurt, July 4 1845
>
> My Dear Sir
>
> Have many thanks for your very kind and welcome letter … and pray tell the members of the committee for the next Festival how truly indebted I feel to them for the honour they have done me in inviting me to come over to their meeting next year.[18]

He continues by saying that he hopes nothing will prevent him from accepting such a "flattering and honourable invitation."

Mendelssohn's reputation for hard work was a quality also much admired. He would not delegate, and was constantly reworking. Edwards tells us that:

> ... after – if not before, or during – the first performance (of Elijah) he discovered numerous instances in the work which could be greatly improved.[19]

This is borne out by the composer himself. In a letter to Klingemann in December 1846, he writes:

> I have again begun to work with all my might at my *'Elijah'*, and hope to amend the greater part of what I thought deficient at the first performance.[20]

But more evidence is to be found, if that were needed, in the fact that soloists and chorus all sang from manuscript copies annotated in the composer's own hand.

Another of Mendelssohn's qualities was his fairness. People who worked with him knew him to be both incorruptible and fair, and this was especially true of his relationship with orchestral players. On one occasion, after a series of problems at an earlier rehearsal in London, the kindly and decent Joseph Moore, the Festival Secretary, wrote to the conductor:

> Nearly the whole Philharmonic band are engaged (for the Festival); a few only are left out who made themselves unpleasant when they were here.[21]

Here he is referring to an incident which had occurred in 1844, when the composer had been engaged to conduct six concerts with the Philharmonic Orchestra at Hanover Square. Apparently, one of the rehearsals had to be abandoned when a small group of players objecting to the repeated rhythmical figures in the long final movement of Schubert's *Symphony No.9 in C (Great)*, withdrew their co-operation and managed to bring the proceedings to a full stop.

It is not a pleasant story. The concert had to be cancelled and one is more than a little amazed that such a thing could have happened. In the circumstances, one is inclined to echo the kindly Joseph Moore's concern – but that Mendelssohn was more interested in the calibre of the players under his baton than his own feelings is clear because he asked Moscheles, his co-conductor at the Festival, to take action. In a letter to him he writes:

> There is nothing I hate more than the reviving of bygone disputes; it is bad enough that they should have occurred in the first place.[22]

He continues:

> If men are to be rejected because they are incompetent, that is my business and I have nothing to say in the matter; but if it is because 'they made themselves unpleasant when I was there', I consider that to be an injustice against which I protest. Any further disturbance on the part of these, I am sure is not to be feared.

The words speak for themselves. That they show great force of character is not surprising. But how many people, one may ask, are so totally devoid of any wish to retaliate for past hurt, especially when to do so is within their brief? Very few.

Another popular aspect of Mendelssohn's personality was his approachability. When asked for help he was usually ready to oblige as he did on the last day of the Festival.

Apparently, just before the final concert, it was discovered that some music was lost and so the composer, who had already taken his seat in the audience, was asked to help. His response was to compose a substitute for the missing Handel Recitative.[23] This he did back-stage 'in a few minutes' producing a piece for tenor solo with accompanying strings and two trumpets. So the band was able to play on and the audience were not cheated of their 'Handel'.

At the time of *Elijah*, Mendelssohn was thirty-six and at the height of his career. He had been a child prodigy and his earliest work was composed at the age of ten – a string trio in time for his father's birthday. After his *'Octet for Strings'* written at sixteen came, in 1826, the following year, his *A Midsummer Night's Dream* overture, an astounding offering from a seventeen-year old. One that has not been rivalled before or since by a composer of that age.

In 1837 Mendelssohn had performed his oratorio, *St Paul*, at an earlier Birmingham Festival. It had met with considerable critical acclaim and did much to establish his reputation as composer, conductor and soloist there and abroad.

The first half of the nineteenth century had seen the rise of the virtuoso instrumentalist. From the 1820's onwards the more dominant role of the conductor was also beginning to emerge. Paganini and Liszt were attracting attention as soloists in the musical capitals of Europe, and the composer/conductor such as Wagner and Mendelssohn were much in demand. Interest in these great men and their music is not without some humour. Paganini's playing was so technically perfect it was thought by some to be supernatural in origin. Unfortunately the Devil was favoured rather than God. Nevertheless this did not deter people from crowding him and trying to touch him in the hope that they, too, might be 'infected' with some of his 'power'.

As we have seen, Mendelssohn's *Elijah* received enormous press coverage. This meant that the orchestra, too, came in for its share of publicity. *The Times* whipped up interest with some personal details about the players and showed a number of them to have been great favourites with the public:

> Old familiar faces met the eye; the veteran Lindley, hugging his violoncello, and cracking jokes with Dr Gauntlett (the concert organist) and the adjoining double bass; Willy's (leader 1st violins) intellectual head and good-humoured smile; Cooke (leader 2nd violins) looking remarkably spruce; Bauman's radiant phiz; and Prospère standing beside his monstre (sic) ophicleide, that resembled in magnitude a pipe of the great organ.[24]

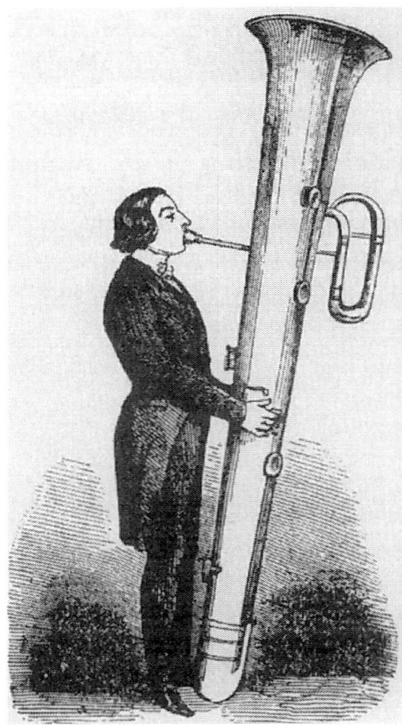

Prospère with his Giant Ophicleide.

Here it is of interest to note that Cooke and Gratton-Cooke were father and son – both well known personalities at the peak of their careers. That Willy, the leader of the Festival Orchestra, was a player of such precocious talent that he had played his first violin concerto in public at the age of seven. Dr Gauntlett, the organist, was another musician of the first class and so one might continue if the point were not already made: that for the premiere of *Elijah*, Mendelssohn directed an orchestra that maintained within its ranks some of the finest musicians in the country.

But to return to that moment when Mendelssohn made his entrance. What did people see?

Although small in stature, he was not more than five-feet six-inches tall and rather slight, he was by no means womanish. His face was extraordinarily expressive – quick to register enthusiasm and if necessary anger. His friend Devrient, leaves this description:

> His features, of the oriental type, were handsome: a high intellectual, and strongly receding forehead; large expressive dark eyes with drooping lids and a peculiar veiled glance through the lashes which sometimes flashed distrust or anger, sometimes happy dreaminess and expectancy. His nose was arched and of delicate form, still more so the mouth with its short upper and full under-lip which was slightly protruding and hid his teeth when with a slight lisp he pronounced the hissing consonants ('S' and 'Z'). An extreme mobility about the month betrayed every emotion that passed therein.[25]

Accounts of Mendelssohn all comment upon the fluidity and range of facial expression. They emphasise the 'Jewishness' of his features and the effect created by his extraordinarily expressive eyes. In the first edition of Grove's *Dictionary of Music*, we get a description of his appearance and character. He was: "Not so much as five-feet six-inches high and slight of build ... very light and mercurial." Grove emphasises: "His mouth ... unusually delicate and expressive," but reserves his greatest admiration for "his large brown eyes." These were "as expressive a pair of eyes as were ever set in a human being's head."[26]

Commenting upon Mendelssohn's personality, Grove is quick to emphasise what it was about the man that made him so attractive to people. He describes his manner as "peculiarly winning and engaging; to those whom he loved coaxing."

Mendelssohn's effect upon women is worth mentioning. "He was peculiarly attractive to women – and ... much sought by them." The composer had numerous women friends as a study of his letters shows. Even so, it is of interest that there is no breath of scandal in his dealings with them. Some may find this refreshing. Mendelssohn's marriage was a great success and his family provided him with the peace and security he needed when out of the public domain. Even so, the opportunities were there in great number, for we must remember that he had the star-billing of a present-day Pavarotti or a Simon Rattle. Again we get this picture of a man ever mindful of what he perceived as the right course of action.

* * * * *

But now it is time and the oratorio is about to begin. At exactly eleven-thirty a.m. Mendelssohn's slight and light figure stepped onto the rostrum. *The Times* takes up the story:

> Mendelssohn … after a brief salutation, waved his baton to begin. Herr Staudigl … delivered in a voice of thunder the awful predictions of the prophet Elijah:[27]

It continues:

> The overture … depicting the despair of the people was magnificently played; the band seemed animated with one magnetic sympathy and it was as though one instrument instead of one hundred and twenty were giving tongue.

The Birmingham Journal has this to say:

> A gentle wave of the baton, but no flood of harmony followed; another, and the stupendous voice of Staudigl as Elijah, was heard prophesying of woes to come. The opening was exceedingly dramatic and the overture that followed, picturesquely descriptive of the sufferings of the Israelites …[28]

The performance which followed, allowing for a twenty-minute interval between parts one and two, should have lasted around two and a half hours. Instead, because of the repeated applause and the numerous encores, there were eight of them, *Elijah* lasted very much longer. Specific passages were repeated at the request of the President, Lord Wrottesley

Herr Joseph Staudigl (1807-1861). The original Elijah in Mendelssohn's Oratorio.

who, if he approved something, signalled to the conductor, probably by lifting his programme.

Both *The Times* and *The Birmingham Gazette* list the titles of numbers encored in this way. Among them was the long chorus *Baal ... we cry to thee*, a choice which the former is quick to point out as "unequivocal proof of (the President's) good taste."

Other encores included: *If with all your hearts, Regard thy servant's prayer, Thanks be to God, He watching over Israel, O rest in the Lord, For the mountains shall depart*, and *O! everyone that thirsteth*.

Whilst to list these is easily done, it is necessary also to try and understand the impression made by them upon the hearts and minds of those present. Not only were the passages enjoyed for their music, but pleasant and pleasing rivalry between the individual soloists and the chorus introduced a new level of anticipatory excitement into the proceedings. Encores were prizes and each in his own way strove to merit one.

No doubt Wrottesley, consciously or otherwise, took his cue from the level of appreciative applause around him, for there were times when the audience 'willed' a repeat and were prepared to carry on clapping until they got one. Edwards talks of "the extraordinary enthusiasm" with which the work was greeted and nowhere is this more obvious than in the wild applause at the end. *The Times* describes the scene:

> The last note of 'Elijah' was drowned in a long-continued unanimous volley of plaudits vociferous and deafening ... enthusiasm ... suddenly burst its bounds and filled the air with shouts of exultation. Mendelssohn, evidently overpowered, bowed his acknowledgement and quickly descended from his ... conductor's rostrum; but he was compelled to appear again, amidst renewed cheers and huzzas.[29]

It continues:

> Never was there a more complete triumph – never a more thorough and speedy recognition of a great work of art.

What is interesting is the universality of the oratorio's appeal. It met with approval at the time, not only from the musical establishment but from ordinary concert-goers as well. Much of the attraction was Mendelssohn himself, as is clear from this extract written by an appreciative member of the public:

> To see (Mendelssohn) conducting was worth anything. He seemed inspired ... the interest that invests that man is quite inexpressible and indeed I never felt (before) the *greatness* of a truly great composer; what are all the performers compared with him?[30]

Whether she realized it or not, this lady in her letter has highlighted a most important point. For what impressed people and what they were delighted to see was Mendelssohn's *control* over the orchestra and choir.

Today this may strike us as extraordinary for that is the very thing that we take for granted. But in Mendelssohn's day, the role of a baton-beating conductor in sole control of an orchestra was a comparatively recent one. Up until around 1820 he had rarely existed, for bands, then much smaller in size, were controlled instead from the keyboard and from the first desk of violins. How it worked was like this. Vocal parts were directed from the organ or harpsichord. At the same time it was the task of the first violinist (the leader) to coordinate the instrumentalists which he did by means of the bow. As orchestras became bigger, this was no longer a sensible idea and it became necessary to invest authority in one man.

The problem was that old customs were difficult to eradicate and rivalry between the keyboard, the leader of the orchestra and the new breed of conductor could, and often did, produce a type of musical anarchy. As recently as 1827, when Mendelssohn first appeared in London before an English audience, he was: "led ... to the piano as if he were a young lady."[31] Even at the *Elijah* concert, much mention is made in the press of the conductor's 'chair' which is clearly a left-over from the past. So, for the audience on that day in August 1846, the sight of a conductor so fully in control as Mendelssohn, was an exciting and rewarding experience.

Bartholomew's libretto was also appreciated. Mention of it in the Festival programme made clear what his aims had been:

> The Author of the English Version of the oratorio of *Elijah* has endeavoured to render it as nearly in accordance with the scriptural texts as the music to which it is adapted will permit.

The result was an edited version of the Old Testament story with which the audience in those days would have been so familiar. His task had been a difficult one. He had to translate from Klingemann's original libretto which was in German. He had to be true to the spirit of the King James' Bible and to produce a work that was structurally sound.

The outcome was something that people could understand; a theme with which they could identify and a story which familiarity rendered enjoyable. To Bartholomew, poet, chemist and personal friend – Mendelssohn acknowledged a considerable debt.

But Bartholomew was not the only one who had worked so hard to help make the performance memorable. Two other men who both in their different ways contributed so much, were James Stimpson, Birmingham choirmaster and organist, and the secretary of the Birmingham Festival,

William Bartholomew (1793-1867).
The English Translator of Mendelssohn's "Elijah".

Mr Joseph Moore. Both will feature prominently in the following chapter, but for the moment it is sufficient to say that without the former's choral skills and the latter's administrative ones, the resultant concert could not have proved the success that it was. At the end of the performance, Mendelssohn would not have grasped Stimpson by both hands and asked him: "What can I give you in return for what you have done for my work?"[32]

Later he was to show his appreciation in a tangible way. The next year he returned to Birmingham to conduct a benefit concert for James Stimpson. He would accept no fee; not even travelling expenses. Such was his gratitude. But to return to the end of the *Elijah* concert. Grove tells of the applause which was: "enormous – almost grotesquely so." Mr Willy, the leader, speaks of the crowds of admirers who sought out the composer afterwards in the artists' room and the eagerness with which they queued to shake him by the hand.

Eventually, an emotionally exhausted Mendelssohn was able to tear himself away. With a few close friends among whose number was Adrian Chorley, the well-known music critic of *The Athenaeum,* he set out to get some air. His humour surfaced. "I'll show you the prettiest walk in Birmingham,"[33] it is alleged that he said as he led the way down to a canal-side walk. Today we would not recognise where they went, for the area has been re-developed and we have Gas Street Basin with its lights, restaurants and brick paving. In Mendelssohn's time however, the way was "bordered by coal and cinder heaps!" Here, oblivious to the dirt and dust of their surroundings, the friends walked for over an hour. Here Joseph Moore tells us that after much animated discussion the composer, already determined upon improvement and refinement of his oratorio, decided to change the duet *Lift Thine Eyes* into a trio.

Joseph Moore's home at the Crescent was nearby, almost within hailing distance of both canal and the Town Hall. Mendelssohn was staying there as he had done on previous occasions and so it is likely that the friends would ultimately have been invited back to continue their talk in more comfortable surroundings.

Upon returning home Mendelssohn writes to his host a glowing letter of thanks. It sheds light on how some of the time between rehearsals and concert was passed. He talks of:

> Quiet morning and evening conversations with Mr Ayrton and Mr Webb (which) ... form an important part of my Musical Festival at Birmingham.[34]

He acknowledges his indebtedness to Joseph Moore:

> I accordingly owe to you the whole of the treat which this first performance of *Elijah* offered me.

And he mentions:

> The friendly reception at your house which enhanced all those pleasures considerably.

Clearly the composer is overtly conscious of the great debt he owes to all the people without whose help his oratorio could have foundered. It is a theme which surfaces again and again in his letters of the time and includes not only the principal actors but each and every member of the choir and orchestra as well.

A letter written to his brother on the same evening expresses these views:

> No work of mine ever went so admirably the first time of execution – nor so good ... or was received with such enthusiasm both by musicians and the audience ...[35]

Now that the Town Hall is briefly empty and the carriages from this concert have returned home with their enthusiastic passengers, it is time to turn back the clock and consider some of the hard work that helped to make this concert the success that it was.

Chapter Four

IN REHEARSAL

Mendelssohn arrived in London on 18 August 1846, to prepare for rehearsals of *Elijah*. He was at the pinnacle of his career and one of the privileged few who were fêted throughout Europe.

Berlioz, Liszt and Paganini (who died in 1842) were all members of this élite and led lives filled with work and travel that leave lesser mortals breathless. They composed, performed and conducted; and had to be continually in the public eye because it was essential that they should not be forgotten by the people who mattered. From Leipzig to London, Berlin to Paris, it was an apparently endless merry-go-round of music making.

The way they lived was not made any easier by the difficulties of travel. At this time the train was little more than a stage-coach on rails. The journey from London to Birmingham often took five hours and the exhaustion of travelling long distances across Europe in draughty bone-shaking compartments must have been taxing.

Mendelssohn's return trip from an earlier visit to Birmingham proves the point. He left straight after a morning concert for London. He arrived there in time to catch the mail-coach to Dover from where he travelled by sea to Boulogne. From there and "without rest of sleep", he continued his journey through Belgium on his way to Cologne. Then it was on to Koblenz where he arrived at three in the morning. After this he had another twelve hours of travel before finally walking through his own front door in Frankfurt. Although this was a decade earlier, travel by train in the 1840's had not greatly improved.

There were also the problems that success brought. These included not only the rigours of travel but the fear of having one's place usurped. Constant vigilance was needed to keep pace with new, younger talent and that was not all. Unlike today, the laws of copyright were in their infancy and compositions still had to be well guarded. Paganini never allowed his trunks out of his sight, and his solo parts were never seen by anyone else.

Musicians like Mendelssohn had to be people of extraordinary physical and mental resource. They had to contend with the weariness of extensive travel and the constant battle against the clock involved in keeping to creative deadlines. They were taxed to extremes. Such a lifestyle would often take its toll. Paganini died at fifty-seven: not by our standards particularly old. Mendelssohn died at the tragically early age of thirty-seven, but what is of importance is that into that short span he packed enough living to make an eighty-year old look back with little regret.

In England as we might expect, Mendelssohn's programme upon arrival was an onerous one. He stayed in London with his great friend, the

Madame Caradori-Allan (1800-1865).
The original soprano in Mendelssohn's "Elijah".

librettist Joseph Klingemann, at 4 Eaton Square. The following day a piano rehearsal for the soloists was to take place at the home of another friend, Ignaz Moscheles, who was also to play and conduct at the Birmingham Festival. This was to be followed by a first orchestral rehearsal booked at London's Hanover Square Rooms.

At the piano rehearsal, delight engendered by the composer's playing of the overture from memory, soon turned to embarrassment brought about by the behaviour of one of the principal sopranos, Madame Caradori-Allan. She is a lady described by H. F. Chorley, the well-known music critic of *The Athenaeum,* as:

> One of those first-class singers of the second class with whom it would be hard to find a fault, save want of fire.[1]

The problem arose with the aria *Hear ye Israel,* which contains a top F sharp. That Madame was having difficulties was soon apparent to all and when she complained that it was not "a lady's song" and made the extraordinary request that the whole aria be transposed a tone down, sympathy evaporated. Later she complained about another of the arias, *O Rest in the Lord*. She suggested the 'improvement' of a long trill on the final note which would result in a 'more fitting' ending.

Mendelssohn's response was to stand firm. Although undoubtedly (and understandably) angry, his manner was one of 'studied politeness'. There could be no transposition and no trill for the soprano which was scored for the flute. This he demonstrated at the piano which was followed by the polite suggestion that should Madame prove unable or unwilling to perform what was required, her contract would be offered to a soprano who was more co-operative.

Although singers were and indeed are privileged and cosseted, there is little doubt that Caradori-Allan's behaviour was extraordinary. Why should she describe what, after all, was a perfectly legitimate soprano aria as not "a lady's part?" How could she imagine that a 'more fitting' ending was necessary? That she was impertinent is not in doubt. The implication, not once but twice, that Madame was a better judge than the composer, of what was and what was not acceptable, is monumental in its arrogance.

But was there more to it than that? Was there professional rivalry or even personal dislike involved? For the facts are that Madame was a second choice for the part, and she knew it. Originally Mendelssohn had Jenny Lind in mind whose voice, with its renowned upper register, would have been more suitable. However, unable to break a previous contract she was not able to sing in the first performance of *Elijah* although she was present when it was performed in Exeter Hall, London, the following year. Jealousy can make people behave in strange ways. Could it have driven Caradori-Allan to present herself as more of a 'lady' than the singer whose place she had taken?

Whatever the reasons were, Mendelssohn was displeased. After the concert he writes to his friend, Livia Frège, about the soprano's performance:

> Along however, with so much light… there were also shadows and the worst was the soprano part. It was all so pretty, so pleasing, so elegant, at the same time so flat, so un-intelligent, so soul-less…"[2]

Fortunately there were no such problems with the other singers, possibly because they were genuinely first-class. Many of them are also of interest in other ways. The great Austrian bass, Herr Staudigl, was not only a great character; he would arrive at rehearsals wearing a stove-pipe hat under which he secreted his copy of the music; he was also the composer's close friend. A most fitting Elijah, he had spent two years at the Benedictine Monastery at Melk before embarking upon a singing career. Later he enrolled as a medical student and it was only when the money finally ran out that he decided to use his great musical talent professionally.

The tenor, John Braham, was also an interesting man. Described by Sir Walter Scott as, "a beast of an actor but an angel of a singer,"[3] he was a writer of numerous popular songs and ballads. As a young man he was befriended by Nelson, and as an older, experienced singer is described in the most glowing terms by Mary Russell Mitford:

> "He is the only singer I have ever heard … who ever conveyed to my very un-musical ears any idea of the expression to which music is susceptible; no-one else joins any sense to the sound. They may talk of music as married to immortal verse, but if it were not for Braham, they would have been divorced long ago."[3]

There are interesting scraps about so many of them. Henry Philips, the other bass, was a keen angler and author of *The True Enjoyment of Angling*; and his *Musical and Personal Recollections During Half a Century* is a rich primary source which opens a window for us on to the Victorian scene. In 1863 he established himself as a singing teacher in Birmingham, and for a number of years accepted students from all over the country.

Of Miss Maria Hawes, one of the principal contraltos, there is little to be said though much to be surmised. She was the daughter of a terror of a father, William Hawes, a prototype of all that would make even the toughest of feminists blanch. A harsh disciplinarian, his daughter would have been subjected to the same rigorous training as the choristers of St Paul's Cathedral where he was Master of the Choristers from 1812 until his death. A man of energy and drive, his house was one where the 'stick' predominated, and his daughter must have been the possessor of a rare spirit in order to rise above and beyond the tyranny of the household. William Hawes died in the February preceding the August of 1846, so by then Maria would have been mistress of her own fate. She did later marry. One can but hope that the husband did not resemble the father.

Then there is the love story of Madame Guilia Grisi (soprano) and Signor Giovanni Mario (tenor). They met in 1839 when she sang the title role in Donizetti's *Lucrecia Borgia*. Mario sang the role of Gerimo and the relationship blossomed from then. Grove tells us that he was eventually to become "her stage partner and life-long companion"[4], a tactful way of describing what in Victorian England would certainly have been considered as "living in sin", before they eventually married.

If all the singers, in Hamlet's words, 'save one' pleased Mendelssohn and they did, there was one young man who especially delighted the composer's ear, and that was the comparatively unknown young tenor, Charles Lockey. Of Lockey Mendelssohn wrote to his brother on 26 August:

> A young English tenor sang so beautifully that I was obliged to collect all my energies so as not to be affected, and to continue beating time steadily...[5]

At this time Lockey was twenty-six years old, the same age as the young choir master, Stimpson, who was to perform such wonders with the chorus.

From then on the singer's name was made, but it is as an advocate for Mendelssohn's *Elijah* that he is to be remembered. That is to say he constantly warned against later over sentimentalised versions of the oratorio that were beginning to creep in and which, it is arguable, were responsible, at least in part, for harsher criticisms of the work which have persisted to this day.

But let's return to that piano rehearsal at Moscheles's house. Some sense of the urgency of the occasion can be gleaned from the fact that all soloists sang from manuscript copies. These had been written out by the librettist, Bartholomew, and were copiously annotated in different coloured pens by Mendelssohn. The latter had been working and re-

Ignaz Moscheles (from a painting by Felix Moscheles). Co-conductor with Mendelssohn in 1846.

working up to the last minute and so there had been no time to obtain printed versions. Singing under these conditions cannot have been easy and one gets a vivid impression of the clock ticking in the background.

But there was much enthusiasm. Mendelssohn at the piano had begun the proceedings, as we have already seen, by playing the overture from memory and this seems to have been the catalyst which animated the rehearsal.

On the following Thursday and Friday, Mendelssohn undertook two of the first full orchestral rehearsals at the Hanover Square Rooms. Although the strain was beginning to tell and he appeared 'worn and nervous', it was now that his enormous capacity for work was demonstrated.

He would delegate nothing; if necessary work far into the night checking the parts. Even so, from the orchestra he obtained full support as is clear from the stories told by those who were there. Nowhere is this made more clear than in the following reminiscence of the clarinettist, Henry Lazarus.

> An instrumental passage in the score for clarinets and flutes was marked 'piano'. In the event, Mendelssohn rapped his stand and asked, "Mr Lazarus, will you kindly make that phrase a little stronger as I wish it to stand out more prominently? I know I have marked it 'piano' (but I do want it heard)." "Of course," replied the clarinettist. "I was religiously playing it as marked."[6]

The operative word here is 'religiously', for it demonstrates how minutely the players were trying to interpret the composer's wishes.

* * * * *

Now it is time to bring Birmingham back into the frame. For while all this activity was taking place in London, much hard work was being carried out up there. Under the directorship of the Town Hall organist and choir master, James Stimpson, the local choir was being rigorously rehearsed.

Stimpson, then a young man of only twenty-six, had already forged a musical career of some interest. He had something in common with Mendelssohn, in that he, too, had been a child with prodigious musical talent. At fourteen he had been considered proficient enough to be left in charge of the organ and choir at Lincoln Cathedral while the organist was away attending a Handel Festival abroad. Later, at the tender age of twenty, he was offered and accepted the post of organist there; but not before at merely sixteen years old, he had for two years been organist-in-charge at St Andrew's Church at Newcastle upon Tyne.

Stimpson was a versatile musician who played the violin as well as the organ. He also composed and was able, like Mendelssohn, to communicate well with other musicians. Described by William Pountney, a long-standing bass singer in the choir, as "a vigorous young man," the organist, too, had a capacity for hard work and painstaking concern for detail. At the time of the *Elijah* concert James Stimpson had been organist at the Town Hall and St Paul's Church for four years, and had achieved a reputation for musical integrity and efficient management.

James Stimpson.

This then was the man entrusted with the onerous and difficult task of training the *Elijah* chorus. A man to whom must be given much of the credit for their magnificent performance, and who was to be rewarded so generously by Mendelssohn the following year.

The well-known Birmingham bass, William Pountney, is of interest not only for his *Memoirs* which present a fascinating eye-witness account of what went on behind the scenes, but also for his remarkable voice which apparently lost little of its virtuosity, timbre and range over a period of almost sixty years: a point taken up by *The Musical Times* of May 1903.

> Mr William Pountney, who sang at the Birmingham Musical Festival in 1846 (when *Elijah* was produced) and on every subsequent occasion (save one) since, has gained admission into the chorus for this year's music-making. We understand that the examiner tried Mr Pountney's bass voice from lower 'D' to upper 'F' and said it was most satisfactory. This length of service is in the nature of a record, and Mr Pountney is to be congratulated on the conservation of his vocal powers.

It is of interest to note that by this time, William Pountney was a man of nearly eighty years old!

Pountney describes Stimpson as, "a smart choir trainer." He continues that, "very little escaped his notice." We learn from him that rehearsals took place at the King Street Chapel, now alas no more, before ultimately being moved to the Town Hall. Discipline was strict and punctuality insisted upon; and for reasons of security choir members were expected to carry with them their contracts or 'engagement papers' at all times. On one occasion this was to prove necessary for Pountney, himself, and two of his friends. They had arrived late and tried to slip in unnoticed. This meant that all three were not subject to the usual checks at the door and that their names were not ticked as 'present'. Their luck was soon to run out for it was not

William Pountney.

long before they were spotted by the door-keeper, a 'burly' and 'imposing' disciplinarian by the name of Parker. "Now what brings you young pippins here?" he is alleged to have roared.

Pountney also tells us how a strike was narrowly averted. Things, it would seem, do not change very much with the passing of the years. Apparently a decision was taken to allow senior members of the choir to sit among the audience when they were not taking part in the performance. Younger men who were not to be granted the same privilege felt aggrieved and decided upon concerted action. They walked out!

And so it was that a very depleted choir turned up for the next rehearsal. However, the orchestral steward, a man of sound common sense, immediately agreed to meet with a deputation of the discontented youngsters. He listened and he acted and the happy outcome was that all the men in the choir might now attend performances when not required to sing. This restored immediate co-operation.

It is unlikely that Mendelssohn would have got to hear about this. Nevertheless, it was an incident of some significance. The circumstances arose out of the young men's involvement with music. It was not more money that they wanted, not even more rehearsal time. What they were requesting was permission to be allowed to make the most of a memorable opportunity which they wished to experience as fully as they could.

In fact, Stimpson and the chorus worked under great difficulty. The problem again was the clock. Mendelssohn's constant revision and re-working of the score meant that there was a good deal of delay. It was not until June that the first instalments of the parts arrived in Birmingham. These were printed and so presented little difficulty. It was with the next set of parts that problems arose because they were all manuscript copies and hedged about with alterations added at different times and in different coloured inks. Those of us who have ever been involved in any sort of creative activity can only sympathise with Mendelssohn and with Stimpson and his choir when presented with this evidence of the anxiety and stress involved in finishing the work to a deadline. The press, too, is not unmindful of the situation:

> The choruses, we may mention, were sent here piecemeal. Mr Stimpson was, consequently, ignorant of the intentions of the composer; but by his apt appreciation of the genius of the work, and his indefatigable

> exertions, it was given with a degree of correctness altogether surprising. A high compliment has been paid to him by the accomplished conductor and the metropolitan press...[7]

The Birmingham Gazette continues by: "willingly (adding) our testimony to the ... well-earned reward."

Not only were the manuscripts difficult to decipher, but things did not always match up. This is illustrated by John Bragg, who was one of the chorus tenors. He says:

> At the passage beginning 'but the Lord' which was an entirely new one for the choralists, Mr Stimpson rapped his desk and asked for the separate voice parts one after another. He then compared them with his own manuscript copy of the score, and being evidently puzzled said, 'Well gentlemen, the voice parts are right and we must sing it so.' And so it was sung... then and ever after: and one of the greatest gems in the work shone out for the first time.[8]

Not all musicologists today would agree with this verdict. But the point is that it represented what the singers at the time believed. It was this that gave them the impetus and courage, stoically to rehearse for long hours because they understood that they were in the process of making history. All those taking part felt the responsibility and the elation of what they were doing. Also, they were not unmindful of the favourable press coverage that they hoped for and were to receive. *The Birmingham Gazette* comments upon, "the successful issue of Mr Stimpson's exertions," and then gives a day by day account of how rehearsals proceeded.

> On Saturday night there was a rehearsal of the principal choruses of the *Elijah* with an organ accompaniment, Moscheles, *who arrived that day* (my italics) conducting.[9]

Covering the proceedings the paper is impressed; and in spite of the fact that there is as yet no orchestra taking part, "finds little difficulty" in discovering "indication(s) of grandeur and dramatic power" in the chorus.

The newly decorated hall again comes in for approval:

> The hall was fully lit up during the rehearsal and the effect was extremely rich without being brilliant. The reddish brown tint of the side panelling, the colour of the seats (cushions) and the red Gothic ornaments of the ceiling, diffuses an extremely warm glow…

As by now we have come to expect, the organ, too, is praised. It is, "chaste yet elaborately decorated," if that were possible, and:

> Two elegant triple lustres introduced on the lower part … bring out the architectural and artistic beauties of this instrument in bold relief.

The following day Mendelssohn arrived in Birmingham. *The Birmingham Journal* reports:

> On Sunday … a special train arrived from London, bringing down Mendelssohn, Staudigl (the bass Elijah), the members of the orchestra, a reinforcement of metropolitan choristers and a cloud of those ubiquitous personages 'gentlemen of the press.'[10]

"Ubiquitous personages" is there not irony here? Or for that matter, rivalry? Perhaps there were times when the local press was less than comfortable with its London rivals. The comment about the 'special train' is also of interest. For while there is no doubt that Mendelssohn did arrive

A locomotive similar to that which Mendelssohn would have encountered.

by train and that it was specially chartered for the occasion, it would not have had the seating capacity to carry the orchestra, soloists, remainder of the choir and so on. In 1846 locomotives were incapable of pulling more than, at the most, six carriages at a time. First-class carriages such as Mendelssohn would have used, sat four passengers only. Second class sat six, but provided only wooden benches to sit on and were open to the skies. It is unlikely that many, if any, of the travellers from London on that day would have used this kind of carriage.

The number of people travelling would have included the band (101), the remainder being local musicians, the London contingent of the chorus (62), eleven soloists, and at least a dozen others to include the critics, among them H.F. Chorley of *The Athenaeum,* and the press. It is clear that all these could not have travelled on one train. Some with Moscheles, Mendelssohn's co-conductor, may have come down on the previous night, but a large number of people are still left. One can only conclude that there must have been a series of trains performing a kind of shuttle operation and that one of these, Mendelssohn's, was singled out for special mention.

The composer set off at two-thirty in the afternoon from Euston Station. His train travelled unusually quickly and what was normally a five hour journey, was completed in four. Trains had no toilet facilities and of course no corridors. So of necessity they were obliged to stop fairly frequently along the route. Perhaps this particular one curtailed some of these stops although we have no means of knowing as records did not begin to be kept until a decade later.

One thing we do know is that Mendelssohn arrived in Birmingham at Curzon Street Station (New Street had yet to be built) at six-thirty in the evening. It is probable that he was met by his old friend, Joseph Moore, with whom he was to stay at his home, The Crescent. Pulled down in 1957, this would have been most conveniently situated as it was within walking distance of the Town Hall. It stood approximately between Cambridge Street and the canal, on land now occupied by Greencoat Tower and Brindley Drive.

Plans for The Crescent, drawn up at the end of the eighteenth century, show it conceived as superior and commodious homes for gentlemen. They are shown as Georgian mews type residences to be built on elevated land with an excellent view over the surrounding area. Unfortunately only houses at each end were ever completed. This was because of the deterioration of the area brought about by the in-filling of land with small

The Crescent, Birmingham, from an engraving by Francis Duke.

workshops, sheds and wharfs. So what we are presented with in Moore's day, are opulent residences in The Crescent where piecemeal industrial development was already beginning to take its toll.

Mendelssohn's full dress rehearsal took place on the following day when it became clear that another problem was looming. The composer had brought with him one fair copy of the full score (the Henschke score)

The Crescent in the 1950's just before demolition.

so called after the name of Eduard Henschke, his Leipzig copyist. He did not, however, bring a copy for the use of Dr Gauntlett, the organist engaged by the Festival Committee for the express purpose of demonstrating the wide ranging potential of their magnificent new organ.

What was to be done? The solution would seem to have been for Mendelssohn to offer Gauntlett his own copy and conduct instead from the version so heavily annotated and coloured – the one upon which he had so recently been working. In what way, if any, did the two scores differ? At any rate, it is clear that one problem had now become two. In the first place, Dr Gauntlett's score now had to be annotated; and in the second, the copy the composer used was probably less clear than it might have been.

However, with such a wealth of good will all round, these difficulties were overcome and Monday, 24 August, was to be remembered, not only as the day a full-page analytical preview was offered in *The Times*, but as one upon which near disaster was turned into a triumph. The triumph of a work awaited with such eager anticipation that even this rehearsal itself was reported by *The Birmingham Journal* which again stresses both the composer's affability and the eager reception of his work:

> Mendelssohn was received by the performers with great enthusiasm renewed again and again, as his lithe and petite figure bent in acknowledgement of those spontaneous and gratifying tributes to his genius, personal affability and kindness ... His manner both in front of the orchestra and in private is exceedingly pleasing. His smile is winning and occasionally when addressing a friendly correction ... full of comic expression ... [11]

A second full rehearsal took place the following day and it seems that the composer in this respect, too, was fortunate. Adequate rehearsal time was what he had asked for and what he had got. In fact there seems to have been only one instance in which the management let him down. Mendelssohn had specifically asked that the performance of *Elijah* should not be followed by anything else. He felt, rightly, that with the completion of his oratorio, the concert should end. From the programme it is clear that his request was ignored. *Elijah* finished. There was then a five-minute interval during which time members of the audience could leave if they wished. Afterwards the band and choir were required to perform a 'selection'. This included one of Handel's *Coronation Anthems* and must have provided an unnecessary and unpleasing anti-climax.

It was not the only time that the conductor's wishes were over-ruled. At a previous Festival, in 1837, Mendelssohn's *St Paul* had been well received. However, a decision taken by the Festival Committee was greeted by the press with more than a little incredulity:

> It was a subject of regret to the great master, and we are sure it would have been the source of very extended chagrin to his admirers, had they been aware of it, to find that the managing committee, under what advice we don't pretend to know, had seen fit to cut out not a small portion of the oratorio (which constituted) some of its best parts.[12]

To substitute a miscellany of pieces of "doubtful merit", which meant that the "noble strains of harmony that pervades Mendelssohn's great work" was not heard in its entirety, was unacceptable.

But on this occasion in 1846 extra rehearsal time was a bonus and work on Tuesday went on far into the night: because as Mrs Moscheles explains, there were still problems with the text. Such was the drama of this testing period.

And so on to Wednesday and the world premiere of *Elijah* which was to make musical history at Birmingham's 1846 Triennial Festival.

Chapter Five

THE CONCERT IN CONTEXT

In order to understand how it came about that Mendelssohn was invited to conduct on a number of occasions at Birmingham's Festivals, it is helpful to take a brief look at how these events came into being. These great Triennial Festivals were not only important as great money-raising events but also for the quality of the music they presented and the talent of the renowned artists prevailed upon to perform. Today they are no longer part of the Birmingham scene. For although money for charity is still raised by private events, much of the burden for fund-raising is now undertaken by taxation. Sunk like the Titanic without trace, these Festivals boast, with every passing year, fewer survivors who can recall the excitement they once engendered.

Initially the Triennial Festivals were conceived in order to help provide the necessary extra money required to maintain a new hospital, the General Hospital, for the people of Birmingham. Lists of possible subscribers, comprising the local gentry, aristocracy and wealthy business men, were drawn up so that they might be invited to buy tickets for these prestigious events. It was understood that they could also donate directly and many of them did.

The necessity for a new hospital had been noted as far back as 1765 by Dr John Ash. Then, the only hospital in existence for the needs of a rapidly rising population had been The Infirmary, a part of the dreaded workhouse, a place where a majority of the many under-privileged were determined not to go.

So, by means of an advertisement in the local press, "the nobility and gentry of the neighbouring country and of the principal Inhabitants of this Town," were invited to attend a meeting at the Swan Inn on November the 24th 1775. Here they discussed "the undoubted benefits of a General Hospital for the relief of the sick and lame ... near the town of Birmingham."[1] This resulted in a list of subscribers being drawn up and a resultant ten-guinea contribution from the 'Musical Society at Sambrooks in Bull Street'. Here is the first evidence of an association between music-making and good causes which was to continue for over a hundred and fifty years and to which Mendelssohn was indirectly a party.

A decision to build was taken, but by 1766 the project had run out of funds. To make matters worse, a scheme to re-build a new Theatre Royal after the old one had burnt down was inundated with donations! Seemingly, entertainment for those who could afford it was considered more important than medical care for those who could not. This at any rate was how a contemporary, the daughter of Mark Wilks, understood the situation. She writes:

> ...whether their (the citizens of Birmingham) generosity expanded at the prospect of self-gratification, whilst it shrunk like the sensitive leave when touched by the subject of charity, it is certain that the theatre was impeded by no pecuniary obstructions, but was rapidly created and completed whilst the hospital stood a miserable object of ruin and dilapidation.[2]

She continues to explain why her father, then a little known bank clerk but later to become a well-known lay preacher, was driven to take the action he did. A sincere Christian, he was horror-struck at what he perceived as an appalling situation. He had little money and less influence; but he had drive and a ready pen which he wielded to good account. He produced his *Poetical Dream*. In this poem an imaginary conversation takes place between a personified playhouse and hospital. The author falls asleep and dreams of what they say. Verse 7 represents the climax of their discussion:

PLAYHOUSE: It must be wrong I do in conscience own
That such unkindness should to thee be shown
That thou by Christians thus should slighted be
Whilst I'm caressed and crowned with dignity.

Later the hospital replies:

HOSPITAL: Sure I this gloomy aspect should not wear
If all were Christians who the name now bear.

His daughter continues:

> He (her father) roused the curiosity and the attention of the public through his poetical talents and by satire (conveying to the inhabitants a picture of their disgraceful negligence as well as a mode of restitution).[3]

It was this "mode of restitution" that is of interest. Wilks sold copies of his poem; (sales in fact went extremely well) and donated the proceeds to the Hospital Building Fund. The success of his poem then enabled Wilks, in his daughter's words again, "(to) set on foot a subscription". She adds that this was extremely successful and that, "in a very short time the hospital was finished and inhabited." Here a little 'poetic licence' is used, for in fact the building was not completed and operational until 1799, the same year that the Birmingham benefactor and industrialist, Joseph Moore, was to stage the first of a series of fund-raising concerts at the Royal Hotel in Colmore Row.

Wilks had blazed a trail, all the more remarkable because of the circumstances in which it had been conceived. The General Hospital was always to prove in need of funds and from now on it is to Moore that we turn, a man who, with his love of music and his considerable administrative skills, was in great part responsible for providing them.

Moore was born in the Worcestershire village of Shelsley Walsh. As a young man, his parents sent him to Birmingham to serve an apprenticeship in the die-sinking trade and there he was to remain for the rest of his life.

A 'die' is a stamp for impressing a design upon softer metal and in non-technical language, he would have been taught how to produce the various patterns which were then 'set' into it. Today we are familiar with rubber-stamps. The process with which Moore was involved would not have been dissimilar but far more technical. At any rate it was a skill that would have proved essential when he later became associated with and eventually a partner in a firm of button manufacturers.

At this time Birmingham was noted for the button trade and many of its manufacturers became wealthy. Joseph Moore, a friend of Matthew Bolton, made a great deal of money which he seems to have used wisely and especially for the benefit of the town and its people. The two men had already discussed the various ways in which music-making could be

Joseph Moore (1766-1851).
Manager of the Birmingham Musical Festivals.

encouraged in Birmingham and this had resulted in the first of a series of concerts staged as mentioned previously, at the Royal Hotel. These are of importance because of the public approval they received, which led to Moore being invited to take on the even greater responsibility of organising the first official Music Festival. Out of this was born the germ of the idea of making these triennial, and so the Triennial Birmingham Music Festivals came into being.

As a means of raising money the Festival Movement was unrivalled. It was popular with the press (very important), the local gentry and the middle-classes. From the first official Festival in 1799, for which Moore both engaged performers and transacted the business, the General Hospital benefited to the amount of £1,470, a sum which today would be worth approximately £70,000.

The Victorian age was competitive. Birmingham's success was noted and other towns and cities responded by organising their own similar events. This led Moore to think in terms of a superior venue in which to house Birmingham's Festivals. He contemplated a building both beautiful and capacious. One that would provide better facilities and enable Birmingham to maintain a premier position within what was now a flourishing festival "league". It was from such beginnings that the idea grew for the eventual building of the town's great Music Hall. But that was to be some way into the future and for the moment the Triennial Festivals continued to be hosted by St Philips.

In 1812, thirteen years after the first concert at the Royal Hotel, Moore was honoured for his contribution to the musical life of the town. This took the form of a presentation of silver consisting of a vase and four covered dishes. It was made on behalf of the committee by Dr Outram, the rector of St Philips, who gave voice to the high esteem in which the benefactor was held.

> We well know, sir, that the flourishing state of that important branch of (the hospital's) revenues which is derived from our Triennial Music Festivals, is to be attributed, in great measure, to your humane, spirited and successful exertions.[4]

He continued by explaining that over the time that Joseph Moore had been associated with the administration of the Birmingham Festival Movement, receipts had risen from two to over six-thousand pounds. He describes the benefactor as, "a private gentleman without any selfish end in view": a concept that today we might have difficulty in understanding.

Moore's reply is also of interest because it throws light upon the kind of man he was. He talks of the General Hospital as, "this great charity," of his own services as, "much too highly appreciated." He then offers, "warmest acknowledgements for the very flattering (and) ... generous sentiments (expressed)."

In spite of these "generous sentiments", Moore's dream of his great Music Hall had to wait until 1832 before coming to fruition. In the meantime he travelled on numerous occasions to many European cities in an attempt to find out how concerts were staged over there. He visited Amsterdam for the express purpose of viewing its great concert hall, and it was ultimately during the time that he was to spend in Berlin that he first met Mendelssohn.

From the beginning the two men liked each other; became and remained firm friends until the composer's death in 1847. It was Moore who was responsible for the commissioning of Mendelssohn's oratorio *St Paul* which was performed in Birmingham in 1837, and of course for the performance of *Elijah*.

In 1832 the decision to erect a Town Hall became policy. Hansom, the architect ultimately engaged, was treated shabbily when funds began to run out and we are presented with a re-run of the General Hospital saga with the Town Hall now in the title role. Work was brought to a standstill; and as at this time there was no Mark Wilks to act as catalyst, Hansom was obliged to shoulder some of the expense himself. Not surprisingly this ultimately ended in his bankruptcy when sadly no heed was taken of his despairing cry for help.

This took the form of his *Appeal to the Rate Payers and Inhabitants of Birmingham* 1834, (3p), in which he tells of being "half frantic with madness" when he realised that the £500 needed to avert calamity, was not going to be forth-coming: "none would assist to avert it." Of the architect, John Foster, to whom the Street Commissioners had originally turned for advice before accepting Hansom's plans, and who was finally brought in to finish the work, he says:

> Who is he? that so ungenerously would claim merit for the Town Hall ... who never used a pencil, spent one anxious thought ... until now when none are needed?

Hansom had literally worked 'day and night' in his desperate attempt to meet deadlines, and it is impossible to read his "A statement of Facts" without feeling sorry for the way he seems to have been treated. The affair has a contemporary flavour and one is uncomfortably reminded of more recent instances when teflon-like the culprit remains at his post and others handle the blame.

What Joseph Moore thought about all this we do not know for he was out of the country for most of the time. Now he was concerned with the building of an organ "at least equal to the finest in Europe", and travelled with his friend, Chevalier Neukom, via Harlem in Holland to Hamburg where the most celebrated organs of the day were made.

In spite of all this, the organ that was eventually commissioned was built back at home in London by Samuel Hill and Son, one of the great organ-building firms of all time. To help raise money for the enterprise, Moore even lobbied the British royal family to obtain "from them and their circle" nearly £2,000. This would be worth around £150,000 today and was nearly half of what the instrument eventually cost.

It can be seen that Joseph Moore was almost single-handedly responsible for the success of the Birmingham Festival Movement. For nearly half a century he was entrusted with the engagement of performers and with the administration of Festival funds. He helped raise enormous sums of money for the benefit of the General Hospital and was instrumental with others in paving the way for both the building of the Town Hall and the inception of its great organ for the people of Birmingham.

If Mendelssohn's passion was his music, Moore's was philanthropy; a wise and discerning benevolence born of education (in his case self-education) and good taste.

If today the concept of good taste is an uneasy one – for one man's opinion we are told, is as good as another's, in the Victorian age this was not so. Self-improvement was encouraged, good taste was to be emulated, lived up to and acquired. Perhaps they were wiser for this view.

Moore and Mendelssohn became close friends in spite of the difference in their ages. Undoubtedly, it was in part because of the kindly treatment received at the hand of the former that the composer, who stayed at The Crescent on his visits to Birmingham, always remembered the town with such affection.

Without Joseph Moore it is possible to argue that *St Paul* would never have been written. For *Elijah* he provided both opportunity and acted as catalyst. The partnership of Moore and Mendelssohn is one to which the Triennial Festival Movement is greatly indebted, as is the General Hospital.

* * * * *

But now to return to the Festival of 1846. Having bade his farewells, Mendelssohn left Birmingham by the seven o'clock train on 28 August, the Friday that the Festival ended, returning to London with Mr and Mrs Moscheles in order to enjoy a fish dinner at Lovegroves that same night.

With his departure the 1846 Triennial Festival was virtually over; except that is, for the customary Ball on the same evening which rounded off the proceedings. This took place at the Theatre Royal New Street and although Mendelssohn was not involved, was a grand affair and is worth a mention.

The dancing took place in a "ballroom" created out of the combined stage and orchestra pit which bad been boarded over to provide ample space for the dancers. The whole area was draped to create the illusion of a tent which, in turn, was lit by three massive and gilded chandeliers suspended from the ceiling. Walls were hung with numerous scenes of oriental exoticism and around the perimeter were a series of miniature fountains which sparkled above basins of flowers and evergreens.

Gala Ball.

The Victorians knew how to do things in style. Even the boxes of the theatre were put to good use. Whilst those adjoining the upper gallery and the gallery itself were open to spectators, the lower were used as "lounges" in which the dancers might relax.

Music for the evening was provided by the well known Jullien, of whom there will be more later, and a "scratch" orchestra which comes in for considerable criticism. "Twenty Julliens cannot turn scrapers into fiddlers" grumbles the press in an indictment soon to be followed by "monotonous" to describe the lack of variety in the programme of dances.

Yet the ladies, with chaplets (wreaths of flowers) in their hair, and dressed in their white or elegantly coloured muslins, are greatly admired: and the "hilarity of the company", together with "the sounds of joyous revelry", lasting well into the night, must all have helped to make this a fitting climax to a Festival week in which Mendelssohn, Moscheles and others had contributed so much.

By Saturday 29 August, the *Birmingham Gazette* is already complaining that information about the takings is as yet hard to come by. It fulminates:

> There is no official account of the results of the meeting yet published and information in that quarter is very difficult to be obtained.

Gathering momentum it continues:

> ... those who are in a position to afford it being so very mysterious and inscrutable, that it is impossible, without an importunity *beneath the dignity of the press* (my italics) to extract anything from them.

How press coverage has changed!

By 7 September, *Aris' Gazette* is able to publish a full list of receipts and donations received. For the Wednesday morning performance, the total amounted to £1,711.11.1. This included bookings for secured and unsecured seats, standing places and donations. However, expenditure was high, so this was not all profit.

Mendelssohn's fee of 200 guineas for attending and 210 guineas for conducting is comparatively modest when it is set against those of the principal soloists. Caradori-Allan received 200 guineas, Grisi asked for 380 guineas and Mario 320. They didn't get it but settled for something in the region of twenty percent less. Cooke, the leader of the first violins was paid

A 'Handel' Recitative by Mendelssohn.

£40 and Willy, leader of the seconds, £20. The chorus were paid £6 each and the London contingent also got free train travel which amounted to an extra pound (see table page).

When the fees of the orchestra are taken into consideration, the violinist Dando, for example, was paid £11, it becomes clear that profit evaporates. So the *Elijah* concert has to be seen within the context of the whole Festival which ended in credit to the tune of £7,402: a sum of approximately £400,000 today: a most laudable achievement.

With Mendelssohn back in London and the Ball over, we sadly take our leave… but not for long as the story remains incomplete without an account of Mendelssohn's return the following year when he came to honour his promise to James Stimpson. It was a promise made, it will be remembered, in the white heat of the moment; at the end of the Festival performance of *Elijah*, in the midst of the clapping and stamping and general excitement. Then, the composer had asked what he might do to repay his friend for Stimpson's dedicated work with the choir, contributing so much to the success of the performance. This was the outcome.

A page from the score Arise Elijah *from Part II.*

This was an earlier Festival (1834) but it shows the crowds and gets the atmosphere that would have prevailed in 1846.

Mendelssohn conducting Elijah (1846). From Illustrated London News 29/8/46.

Chapter 6

THE RETURN

So it was that Mendelssohn agreed to conduct the revised version of his oratorio at a benefit concert for his colleague; an occasion on which only Birmingham Festival Choral Society (BFCS) members were to be involved. Not only this, but as already mentioned, such was the measure of the man he would take no fee and did not even charge for his expenses. For Stimpson was in need of money and the composer determined to use his name to see that the choirmaster obtained it.

Why did a successful, young organist and choirmaster like Stimpson need more money? Too many facts can read like a cookery book, but a glance at the musician's exemplary career will make clear why this benefit concert was necessary. Born in 1820, he had entered Durham Cathedral Choir School as a chorister at the age of seven: and when his voice broke his considerable talent upon the organ was put to good use instead. Indeed, such was his prowess that at the early age of fifteen, he was deemed competent to deputize for the sick organist of Carlisle Cathedral, becoming organist-in-charge there at twenty-one when the incumbent died. Then in 1842, it was on to Birmingham where the committee unanimously appointed him to the post of Town Hall organist and organist of St Paul's Church in Hockley.

So did James Stimpson become a lively contributor to Birmingham's musical life: one that enabled him to meet and make music with some of the world's top class instrumentalists and conductors. Birmingham was also a place where he was able to develop his own skill with the baton.

In 1845, Stimpson had started his Monday evening concerts, later to be known as "Mr Stimpson's Concerts Monstres" (sic), a name with a clue as to their length! Victorian audiences were used to enjoying, we might say enduring, concerts of well over three hours. The programmes were devised to appeal to as wide an audience as possible and included a good deal of "light" music. Items such as Jullien's *Masurka Quadrille* or his *The Cricket Polka* which had nothing to do with the sport and was a piece inspired by Dickens'

The Cricket on the Hearth, were especially popular. Later programmes were to spread the net more widely, to include Auber's overture, *La Bacarolle*, and operatic selections from Mayerbeer's *Robert Le Diable*.

For over a decade Stimpson continued to offer such musical offerings to his public – but from early on they were to become a financial drain. The musicians and the soloists had to be paid – and frequently the choirmaster was obliged to make good the shortfall out of his own pocket. This puts Mendelssohn's appearance at the former's benefit concert into context; also his refusal to accept a fee, a generous gesture which meant that even after expenses, Stimpson would have been able to remain financially solvent for some time to come.

Sadly though, and in spite of the composer's excellent intentions, it was soon to be apparent that this occasion was in many ways different from the performance of the previous year. Mendelssohn's health, and the absence of a Festival Committee; limited funding and grossly inadequate rehearsal time were all to play their part in determining an outcome less auspicious than that of 1846.

On this return visit Mendelssohn's "diary" would have looked something like this:

12 April.	1847.	Arrive Klingermann's, Hobart Square, London.
16 April.	"	Conduct *Elijah*, London's Exeter Hall.
20 April.	"	Conduct *Elijah*, Manchester.
23 April.	"	Conduct *Elijah*, Exeter Hall.
26 April.	"	Philharmonic Society. Conduct, *A Midsummer Night's Dream, Symphony no.3. (Scottish)*. Perform Beethoven's *G Major Concerto*.
27 April.	"	*Elijah*, Birmingham.
28 April.	"	*Elijah*, Exeter Hall.
1 May. a.m.:	"	Prussian Embassy.
p.m.:	"	Buckingham Palace.
4 May. a.m.:	"	Beethoven Quartet Society.
p.m.:	"	Antient Concert – organ recital.
6 May. a.m.:	"	Lord Ellesmere's Picture Gallery.
p.m.:	"	Prussian Embassy – recital.
9 May.	"	Calais and home.

It is a "diary" demonstrating even to the most cursory observer that by now, the composer was in the process of literally working himself to death. One that provides a record of the Birmingham *Elijah* on 27 April "sandwiched" between a concert in London, both the day before and the day after.

This was to have repercussions. It meant that time was very limited – a matter of considerable importance – as the revised oratorio would need more rather than less rehearsal time.

Just how rushed Mendelssohn was is clear from his own pen. "My time," he writes from Manchester to his host, Joseph Moore, in Birmingham:

> Will be very limited as I must assist at the Philharmonic Concert in London on the 26th and conduct there my "*Elijah*" on the 28th again.

Then, and after thanking Moore for his "kind note", he details his schedule. He will:

> Arrive in Birmingham just in time to go to the Town Hall, and rehearse at half past one, and must leave Birmingham on the next day at half past nine.[1]

He proposes to get to Moore's home in the Crescent *immediately* after the rehearsal, where he looks forward to, "a quiet chat... after the concert or the next morning". A hope that one cannot help feeling was optimistic. The concert was scheduled to start at seven thirty in the evening and, in the event, was to end at ten forty-five when applause and farewells would take a further toll upon what was left of the day. Mendelssohn's early start from Curzon Street Station the next morning would not have allowed much time for relaxation either.

Mendelssohn travelled first class for the four hour journey back to London, where he arrived at one-thirty p.m. in time for another afternoon rehearsal, prior to conducting *Elijah* again that same evening. It is a train of events that makes one breathless even to recount. A time-table which would have tired even the fittest of men, which at this time the composer certainly was not.

According to W.S. Rockstro, a pupil of the Maestro from Leipzig, "There can be no doubt that (Mendelssohn's) health was, by this time seriously, if not hopelessly impaired." Rockstro dates the beginning of this final decline from the time of the first performance of *Elijah* eight months previously when he had first become aware of "a worn look quite foreign to his usual expression". At first he points out this was noticed only by intimates, but now it had become "more pronounced and patent to everyone."[2]

But overwork was not the only problem. That there was some sort of genetic weakness is also without doubt and what was being witnessed here were the initial stages in the countdown to Mendelssohn's tragic, early death in November 1847. Fanny, the composer's beloved sister was also to die young. She did not regain consciousness after a stroke in May 1847 – the final blow that caused Mendelssohn irreparable emotional damage. All would seem to have played their part in a pattern of disasters from which he could not escape and which were first hinted at in Birmingham. A sombre thought, because it means that the triumph of *Elijah* has links, however tenuous, with the end of the composer's life.

All that a layperson can do is to relate what was to happen later: that soon after a brief holiday in Switzerland and his return home, the composer's attacks of violent headaches and intermittent lapses into unconsciousness became more frequent. That on 3 November, 1847, he lapsed into a coma from which he never recovered, dying at a quarter to ten in the evening of the following day.

A most likely cause of death is provided by Dr Evan Bedford, one time Consultant Physician to the Middlesex Hospital. He suggests that Mendelssohn died of a "subarachnoid haemorrhage from a congenital cerebral aneurysm which leaked on several occasions prior to the fatal (attack)."[3] All of which points to the fact that the composer was in no fit state to undertake the gargantuan work load that he shouldered during his final trip to England. It is arguable that those reserves of energy which might have enabled him to deal more comprehensively with problems in Birmingham as they arose, were depleted. Even so, an indomitable will; his ability to mesmerise by means of "those dark lustrous unfathomable eyes... black, but... shining, not with a surface light, but with a pure serene, planetary flame...", saw him triumphantly through – as did his spellbinding leadership from the rostrum where he was now viewed as:

> ...a man of small frame, delicate and fragile looking; yet possessing a sinewy elasticity and power of endurance which you would hardly suppose possible.[4]

In Rockstro's words, "Ill and aged" he may have looked to those around him, but there is evidence that Mendelssohn, himself, was only too aware of his precarious situation. His reply to a request that he should prolong his stay in England, "One week more of this unremitting fatigue and I should be killed outright"[5], says it all.

If the composer's health gave cause for concern, limited rehearsal time, mentioned earlier, was a problem even more immediate. For the score on this occasion, was the revised version of *Elijah*: the one we know today and greatly changed from the earlier version.

Indeed how changed can come as rather a shock: and whilst it is not the intention here to discuss these alterations at length, a few examples will make the point. Of the forty-two arias throughout the work, eleven are either re-scored or extensively altered, including the opening and closing choruses. And whilst the former is now greatly extended, the latter, "...remodelled and improved thereby... altogether different, more massive and elaborate"[6], is also greatly approved of by the press. Note is also taken of the libretto which shows, "striking evidence of a careful and critical revision;" a welcome comment, demonstrating how seriously this critic takes his job, when frequently reviewers make (and made) no mention of anything other than the music.

Then there is that beautiful aria, *Lift Thine Eyes*, originally a duet and now a celebrated trio. A change, it will be remembered, already dimly envisaged along that memorable canal side walk, when Mendelssohn with Moore and Chorley were all three "fizzing" with excitement from the success of the oratorio's premiere. So it is clear that these and all those other momentous changes, would have needed more rather than less rehearsal time if the performance were not to suffer: sadly, a common state of affairs both then and today.

Added to limited rehearsal time, was the problem of the missing soloists and players. An extra burden was placed upon the conductor by the fact that the occasion was to be deprived of a number of "star" performers, their places to be taken by less experienced musicians.

Of all the soloists present, only Mr Lockey had sung on the previous occasion and the absent Staudigl was greatly missed. "What no Staudigl?" writes Mendelssohn to Joseph Moore in a tone of surprised disappointment a mere few days before the concert.

Instead, Elijah was to be sung by Mr Philips who, although he turned out to be "an excellent substitute, (could) not bear a favourable comparison with Staudigl." Especially, the newspaper continues:

> When attempting the massive music... which constitutes the air *Is not his Word like Fire*? (only) Staudigl alone, of any vocalist we have heard can roll this forth with fullness of tone and breadth, yet sharpness of stocatto (sic), that give the music its distinguishing character.[7]

By comparison, it is unlikely that the absent Madam Caradori-Allen, whose part was substituted by Miss Birch, a singer popular with Birmingham audiences, and who exhibited "a vigour and freshness (which) evinced a nice appreciation of the composer's intention" – was missed at all!

Not only were "star" vocalists missing. The depleted orchestra was also bereft of well-known instrumentalists. Contrary to some reports, Mr Willy was not present to lead the band with Mr Thomas Cooke. Neither was Gratton-Cooke, who on the previous occasion had been the principal oboe. *The Dramatic and Musical Review* is quick to point out the resultant disappointment of the programme's unfulfilled promises:

> The programme stated that the orchestra would be comprised of the élite of the London profession, and of all the talent that could be procured in the town and neighbourhood. The "elite" of the London profession was represented by Mr T Cooke and Mr Harper – (and only) a few other – members ... of whom I have any knowledge.[8]

So it would appear that Mendelssohn was to conduct on that night a "scratch" orchestra – depleted and vastly less experienced than the band which the composer had so triumphantly directed eight months previously. Players who, with the exception of Mendelssohn, himself, were to be mercilessly exposed in the press. *The Dramatic and Musical Review* is especially critical:

> The band was inefficient and showed a complete want of unity and precision, it went on straggling and blundering through the music, evidently causing Mendelssohn much pain, as well as trouble in keeping it together.

The Athenaeum, represented by the pen of Adrian Chorley, friend and great admirer of the composer, also weighs in. What he has to say concerning the following day's London performance of the oratorio might as well have been written for the Birmingham one. First come the compliments as the "admirable elevation and spirituality" of the oratorio are discussed. It is a work free from: "the slightest admixture of secular levity of sanctimonious foppery," surely a glorious phrase if there ever was one! Then comes the dilemma: the choice between self esteem and reputation: between "well intentioned amateurs" and the "reputation of a great work." His decision to speak "unpalatable truth," is a task that he proceeds to set about with a will. He castigates both "the incorrectness of the choralists and the meagreness and vacillation of the band", which together serve so "as entirely to confuse outline, form, texture, light and shade, throughout the greater part of the work".[9] A criticism that is arguably misdirected, and could have been focused instead upon the wholly inadequate rehearsal time.

Finally Chorley poses the question as to why nothing better was placed "at the disposal of Europe's greatest composer?" Why indeed? Why, back in Birmingham, were important names like that of Dr Gauntlett missing? A musician whose role on the organ was taken over by Stimpson, himself, "very ably" and who is consistently praised "for the spirit displayed in projecting and carrying out so magnificently an undertaking".[10]

Eight months previously Stimpson had turned the pages of Gauntlett's score: now he was admirably to deputize. And yet the fact remains that however excellent his performance, Stimpson was not Gauntlett, the composer of hymn tunes and chants that "are numbered in thousands"; whose career as a successful solicitor was only surpassed by his brilliance as an organist – a "star" in his own right and much admired, in spite of his "tricky" temper, by Birmingham audiences. It must be faced, that without the presence of Dr Gauntlett this benefit concert lost a little of its gloss, for what is **perceived** in life often matters more than what **is**.

So many old favourites – so many "star" names missing and one returns with Chorley to that question why? Many were Mendelssohn's friends, after all, and one must assume that on a personal level they would have wanted to be in Birmingham on that night. Without doubt, their presence would have made the composer's task much easier.

Missing records due to a library fire in 1879 and later, bomb damage during the Second World War, make research difficult. But clearly there was a problem with finance as "big" names would have been entitled to large fees that Stimpson would not have had the resources to pay.

Then there is that sense of hurry, a general haphazardness that poisoned the arrangements: Mendelssohn, for example, learning, almost on the eve of the performance, that Staudigl would not be taking the leading role (although the latter did perform for the conductor in London the next day). And should this be dismissed as surmise, it is undoubtedly a fact that Mendelssohn conducted on that night in circumstances less than favourable and that the ensuing emotional and physical cost to him was very great.

In general terms, this is how it was: but now is the time for a closer look at the event from inside the Hall on that night.

Dr Henry John Gauntlett, 1875. By kind permission of the National Portrait Gallery.

Chapter Seven

MR STIMPSON'S BENEFIT CONCERT

Again the press sets the scene and it is no surprise to find that attention first focuses upon the audience:

> The side and great galleries were adorned with the rank and fashion of the town and neighbourhood, and the company on the floor formed a fitting pedestal to this Corinthian Capital.

Upon closer scrutiny, however, it is clear that all is not quite as it seems:

> The greater part of the Hall was reserved; these seats with *few solitary exceptions* were filled and every *comfortable corner* of the unreserved quarters had its due proportion of occupants.[1]

So the seats were **not** sold out – not even for Mendelssohn- and in spite of the Festival Concert eight months before, when the aisles and gangways were packed with people "camping" there on seats that they had brought out from home. Neither the reserved nor the unreserved seats were fully booked, although undoubtedly by usual standards the audience would have been considered robust.

But was it well behaved? Apparently not, as a letter of 28 April to *Aris' Gazette* makes clear. In it, the writer, who signs himself "an amateur", refers to "a most intolerable nuisance" which turns out to have been "the loud and continued talking of 'gentlemen' behind". Furthermore, he also complains of people leaving the auditorium before the performance is finished:

> It would also be a common respect to Dr Mendelssohn, or any other Composer whose music is being performed, if those who are weary of the piece before it is brought to a conclusion would be considerate enough to

> sit it out. The confusion of leaving their place, being as bad a compliment to the composer as it is an intolerable disturbance to musical amateurs.

So it would seem that loutish behaviour, then as now, had the same potential to disrupt and to destroy other people's pleasure.

It is unlikely that Mendelssohn would have been aware of what took place within the body of the Hall. At least, one hopes he was not, and the praise that was to be lavished by the press upon the quality of his revised score would, in any case, have provided him with solace. But this is to run on ahead and the concert is only just about to start.

At precisely half-past seven – for Mendelssohn was meticulously punctual – "the great composer mounted the rostrum amid repeated salvos of applause": and as the oratorio got under way, there was much to enjoy. Of special interest was the introduction of a new character, Obadiah, sung by Mr Lockey who combined the role with the two tenor airs: *Then Shall the Righteous* and *If With all your Hearts* which he had performed at the Festival. Obadiah is a dramatic devise for providing a connecting link between incidents, such as the destruction of the prophets of Baal, Elijah's prayer for rain – and the boy who is sent to the seashore to await God's hoped and prayed for, aid. The critics loved it – but ever mindful of the composer's genius are careful to point out that:

> The want of a connecting link might never have been noticed but for the critical eye of the composer, and as it is a manifest improvement we have this additional proof of his poetic taste.[2]

With such goodwill from the press eager to record success: the recounted encores of Miss Dolby's rendering of *O Rest in the Lord*, for example, and Miss Birch's "brilliant roulades"; Mr Lockey's "sweetness and chasteness" of expression; it is sad that, overall, the performance of the oratorio was let down by the ineffective playing of the orchestra, "smaller and less select" than might have been expected. There were also doubts in some quarters, concerning the chorus, "more powerful than expressive".

Now while it is true that the "electrifying" effect of the Festival *Elijah* was never likely to be repeated, for there can never be more than **one** first performance; it is surely unfortunate that on this second occasion, offered by Mendelssohn with such good intent, there should have been more than a "whiff" of disappointment in the air; and this because the composer was obliged to "make do" with second best.

But the composer's own musical integrity was never in doubt and the concert ended well with Mendelssohn "applauded to the echo" as he stepped down from the rostrum to bid his friends and his fans goodbye for the final time. Nobody else could have achieved more and he had triumphed by keeping the orchestra together in circumstances that would have proved impossible for a lesser man.

So it was that later that evening, an exhausted Mendelssohn and his friend, Joseph Moore, returned to the latter's Crescent home. The two men were never to meet again and with hindsight, the little time that was left to them was therefore especially poignant. The two friends, always at ease in each other's company, would no doubt after all, have found time for "the quiet chat" that the composer had earlier envisaged – and for refreshment and for some little ease. But the clock would have been ticking and by early the following morning, Mendelssohn's mind would have been set upon his next London engagement.

Then it was not to be long before on 9 May he was to return home to Leipzig – never again, as has already been noted, save for a brief holiday in

Mendelssohn's home in Leipzig. Photograph by Geoffrey Duggan.

Switzerland to leave his native Germany. So was this performance of his revised *Elijah* to mark the end of a long and memorable association with Birmingham. A partnership that was to have lasted for over a decade.

He had first appeared on the Birmingham scene in September, 1837, when he was invited to direct that year's Music Festival and to conduct his oratorio, *St Paul*. Such was his success, mirrored in an enormous upsurge of takings at the box office, that he was invited to return to the city again in 1840, both to direct the Festival and to conduct his *Lobgesang Op52* – better known today as *Symphony No2, The Hymn of Praise*. It is a work described by Pountney as a "symphonic cantata" and all agree that it was written to be first performed at the Thomaskirchen in Leipzig.

A study of the takings reflects just how popular the composer was. The year, 1843, when Mendelssohn was unable to attend because of other commitments, shows a marked drop in the money earned. But net takings doubled in 1846, when he again returned to the helm. Pountney tells us that there were other considerations as well. The conductor for the Festival in 1843 was Mr Kinjvet who had conducted at a number of the earlier Festivals; and it would appear that on this occasion, his decision to include Rossini's *Stabat Mater* in the programme had "excited a vast amount of displeasure among the local clergy." In fact, the influential rector of St Martin's in Birmingham's Bullring, Mr Moseley, even went so far as to denounce the work as "idolatrous and anti-Christian!" So have the times changed.

But with Mendelssohn's return all this was forgotten; and the story of the premiere of *Elijah* in Birmingham is to be seen as one of the brightest 'gems' of the city's Festival tradition. A story to be savoured and with it the memory, not only of the composer, but of Mr Joseph Moore, one of the kindliest of benefactors. Moore who was administrator and facilitator of Birmingham Festivals for almost fifty years and whose portrait, recently renovated, one might hope will one day hang where it surely belongs – in the newly refurbished Town Hall. He is a man whose friendship with Mendelssohn epitomises all that can be achieved when administrative skill and poetic genius come together for the greatest good. Two men and a partnership of which Birmingham is justly proud and to whom it is now time to bid farewell as they say their 'goodbyes' before Mendelssohn sets off on his journey to London for the final time.

TABLE OF FEES

	1846	2011
Mendelssohn	200 guineas	£15,015
Mendelssohn	£200	£14,300
Staudigl	£150	£10,725
Braham	£50	£3,575
Dr Gauntlet	£30	£2,145
Cooke	£40	£2,860
Willy	£20	£1,430
Dando	£11	£787
Chorus	£6 + £1 Expenses	£501
Moscheles	£100	£7,150
Caradori-Allan	200 guineas	£15,015

It can be seen from the above table that Mendelssohn received two fees: the first was for attending the Festival and the second was for conducting. Both are comparatively modest, especially when compared with the amount of money paid to the principal singers.

POSTSCRIPT

The score of the original version of *Elijah* used by Dr Gauntlett at the first performance is now in the possession of the Archive Department at Birmingham Central Public Library. The oratorio's reputation has had a chequered history as has Mendelssohn's own.

At first *Elijah* was greatly applauded and regarded by the concert-going public as the height of fashion. It was a great 'crowd-puller.' Then it fell out of favour with the musical establishment, possibly because of the over-sentimentalised versions that came to be presented as the norm. More recently its reputation has revived; for it was and remains a work of great dramatic appeal. A point that is illustrated both by its successful performance in costume at the Albert Hall before the outbreak of the Second World War and the more recently re-issued version on compact disc of the Fischer-Dieskau / Janet Baker version of the 1960's.

So much for the oratorio: but what of the Town Hall where it was first performed? Today, after many setbacks, it has been restored to its former glory and the story of how this was achieved is one of dogged persistence and undimmed aspiration.

Having been Birmingham's pride for over a century and a half, by the mid 1990s this once magnificent building was badly in need of repair. In December 1995, *The Birmingham Mail* revealed it to be a danger to the public, its doors fitted with safety nets to prevent masonry falling on passers by!

Numerous lottery bids were to prove unsuccessful but, ultimately, with the aid of money from the European Regional Development Fund (£3 million), the Heritage Lottery Fund (£13.7 million) and capital provided by Birmingham City Council itself (£18.3 million), which together provided a grand total of £35 million, restoration work was at last able to begin and be successfully completed.

On Thursday, 4 October 2007, the Hall re-opened to a barrage of publicity and a fortnight of celebratory events, providing the perfect setting for organ and piano recitals as well as chamber music and choral works.

During its long life the Town Hall has played host to many interesting and extraordinary events. In 1853 Dickens gave his first reading of *A Christmas Carol*. In 1901 Lloyd George, whose silken tongue proved unable to work its usual magic, was obliged to leave by a side door in the guise of a policeman to avoid the anger of a hostile crowd.

Among musicians, Mendelssohn is one of a great roll call. However, his appearance was important in other ways. It increased the prestige of the Triennial Festival Movement and encouraged many of the most celebrated artists to visit the town in the future. The *Elijah* concert was a watershed in Birmingham's musical life, an important aspect of which was to be resumed with the re-opening of the Town Hall and the resumption of concerts there. Now hopefully a visit to the 170 year old building will again provide the 'sense of occasion' that it once did.

Interior shot of the recently restored Birmingham Town Hall. Photograph by Mike Gutteridge.

CHAPTER NOTES

Chapter 1

1. Hutton p386.
2. Pemberton, *The Monthly Repository*, Feb 1835.
3. Skip, p78.

Chapter 2

1. The Festival of 1837.
2. *The Times*, 26 August.
3. See p64.
4. *Birmingham Gazette*, 26 August.

Chapter 3

1. *Aris' Gazette*, 24 August 1846.
2. *London Illustrated News*, 29 August 1846.
3. *The Times*, 26 August 1846.
4. There were other lavatories; male urinals outside and a second water closet along the west corridor which complements one on the other side of the building. It is not known whether ladies would have had access to this.
5. Grant p78.
6. "A type of brass consisting of three parts copper and two parts zinc used in casting." Collins Dictionary.
7. Grove, Vol 2, 1st edition p283.
8. Ibid, p227.
9. Edwards, p82.
10. Ibid, p80.
11. *Grimshaw Letters*.
12. *The Times*, 25 August 1846.
13. Edwards, p82.

14. Ibid, p79.
15. Edwards, p80.
16. Ibid, p80.
17. *Birmingham Journal*, 24 August 1846.
18. Edwards, p30.
19. Edwards, p97.
20. Ibid, p97.
21. Ibid, p43.
22. Edwards, p43.
23. Recitative which precedes the final chorus of Handel's *Zadok the Priest*.
24. *The Times*, 26 August 1846.
25. Devrient, p236.
26. Grove, Vol 2, 1st edition, p273.
27. *The Times*, 26 August 1846.
28. *Birmingham Journal*, 26 August 1846.
29. *The Times*, 26 August 1846.
30. Edwards, p90.
31. Grove, Vol 2, 1st edition, p263.
32. Edwards, p84.
33. Ibid, p84.
34. Ibid, p92.
35. Ibid, p85.

Chapter 4

1. New Grove, Vol 3, p768.
2. Edwards, p87.
3. New Grove, Vol 3, p155.
4. Grove, Vol 2, p689.
5. Edwards, p86.
6. Ibid, p78.
7. *Birmingham Gazette*, 22 August 1846.
8. Edwards, p46.
9. *Birmingham Gazette*, 24 August 1846.
10. *Birmingham Journal*, 25 August 1846.
11. *Birmingham Gazette*, 1837.
12. *Birmingham Journal*, 23 September 1837.

Chapter 5

1. Bunce, p10.
2. Ibid, p11.
3. Bunce, pp12/13.
4. Langford, Vol 2, p321.

Chapter 6

1. Polko, p244.
2. Todd, p544.
3. *Music and Letters*, Vol 36, p376, 1955.
4. Todd, p494.
5. Stratton, p128.
6. *Birmingham Journal*, 28/4/1847.
7. Ibid.
8. *Dramatic and Musical Review*, Vol 6, p224, 1847.
9. *The Athenaeum*, 1847, p441.
10. *Birmingham Journal*, 28/4/1847.

Chapter 7

1. *Birmingham Journal*, 1/5/1847.
2. Ibid.

Appendix 1

BIBLIOGRAPHY

Books

Benedict, Julius: *A Sketch of the Life and Works of the Late Felix Mendelssohn Bartholdy*, (London 1850).

Blunt, Wilfred: *On Wings of Song*, (London 1974).

Bunce, Wilfred J.T.: *The Birmingham General Hospital and Triennial Music Festivals*, (Birmingham 1858).

Campbell, Margaret: *The Great Violinists*, (London 1980).

Carse, Adam: *The Orchestra from Beethoven to Berlioz*, (New York 1948).

Dent, R.K.: *The Making of Birmingham*, (London 1894).

Dent, R.K.: *Old and New Birmingham*, (London 1973).

Devrient, Eduard: *My recollections of Felix Mendelssohn-Bartholdy and Letters to me*. Trans. Macfaren, (London 1869).

Edwards, F.G.: *The History of Mendelssohn's Oratorio Elijah*, (London 1896).

Elvers, Edward, ed: *Mendelssohn a Life in Letters*, (London 1896).

Freeman, Michael and Alcroft, Derek: *Transport in Victorian Britain*, (Manchester 1988).

Garland, Henry and Mary: *The Oxford Companion to German Literature*, (OUP 1985).

Gill, Conrad: *History of Birmingham*, (OUP 1952).

Grant, James: *Portraits of Public Characters*, (London 1841).

Grove, Sir George ed: *Dictionary of Music and Musicians*, (London 1878-1890).

Hanford, Margaret: *Sounds Unlikely*, Birmingham and Midland Institute, (Birmingham 1992).

Hopkins, Eric: *Birmingham the First Manufacturing Town*, (London 1989).

Hutton, William: *Birmingham*, (Birmingham 1882).

King-Smith, Beresford: *Crescendo*, (London 1995).

Langford, John Alfred: *A Century of Birmingham Life*, (Birmingham 1868).

The Oxford Companion to Music, London 1938.
Polko, Elise: *Reminiscences of Felix Mendelssohn-Bartholdy*, (London 1869).
Radcliffe, Philip: *Mendelssohn*, (London 1954 revised 1976).
Rockstro, W.S.: *Mendelssohn*, (London 1884).
Scholes, Percy A.: *The Mirror of Music 1844-1944*, (London 1944).
Skipp, Victor: *The Making of Victorian Birmingham*, (Brewin Books 1996).
Stratton, Stephen S: *Mendelssohn*, (London 1934).
Sutcliffe-Smith: *The Story of Music in Birmingham*, (Birmingham 1945).
Todd, Larry: *A Life in Music*, (OUP 2003).
Yarwood, Doreen: *Victorian and English Costume*, (London 1985).

Archive Material

Edge Plans and Specifications for Birmingham Town Hall, (1848).
Grimshaw Letters, M/S, (1834).
Mendelssohn Score of *Elijah*, M/S, (1846).
Pountney, William: *A History of the Birmingham Music Festivals*, M/S, (1899).

Other Sources

AKG The Arts and Picture Library, London.
Aris's Gazette.
Dramatic and Musical Review, Vol 6, 1847.
The Architectural Magazine, Vol 2.
The Athenaeum, 1846/1847.
The Birmingham Conservatoire (library), University of Central England.
Birmingham Post and Mail.
The Birmingham Gazette.
The Birmingham Journal.
Burke's Peerage.
Cokayne, A Complete Peerage.
Crockford's Clerical Dictionary.
Curator of Costume, Walsall Museum and Art Gallery.
Dictionary of National Biography.
The Gentleman's Magazine, Vol 190, (Jan/June 1851).
Office of National Statistics London.
Music and Letters, Vol 36, 1955.

Pemberton, Reece: *The Monthly Repository*, (February 1835).
Royal Astronomical Society, London.
Royal Military Academy, Sandhurst.
Royal Military School of Music, Kneller Hall.
Royal Philharmonic Society, London.
Scribner's Magazine: *Mendelssohn's Letters to Moscheles*, Vol 13, (1888).
Solihull Public Library.
York Railway Museum.

Appendix 2

PERSONALIA

BARTHOLOMEW, William (1793-1867)
Chemist, violinist and flower-painter. Best known as translator/adaptor of Mendelssohn's works including: *Antigone*, *Oedipus* and *Elijah*.

BENNETT, Sir William Sterndale (1816-1875)
English composer and friend of Mendelssohn. Founded Bach Society 1849. Conductor Philharmonic Society (1856-1866). Professor of Music Cambridge University (1856). Principal Royal College of Music (1866).

BRAHAM, John (1774-1856)
English tenor and composer. Appeared in *The Messiah* at Birmingham Triennial Festival 1846. Relinquished his part in *Elijah* to the tenor Charles Lockey.

CARADORI-ALLAN, Maria (1800-1865)
Italian born soprano. Settled in England. London début 1825 as soloist in first performance of Beethoven's *Choral Symphony*.

CHORLEY, Adrian Henry Fothergill (1809-1889)
Journalist, author, art-critic for *The Athenaeum*. Criticism included music and literature. Wrote Coleridge's obituary.

COOKE, Thomas (Tom) Simson (1782-1848)
Born Dublin. Gifted violinist, opera singer and composer. First public performance, violin concerto aged seven. Leader of band, Crow Street Theatre, Dublin at 15. Principal tenor, Drury Lane Theatre, London 1815-35. Leader second violins *Elijah* Birmingham, 1846. Died London.

Cooke-Gratton, Henry Angelo Michael (1804-1889)
Professor of oboe Royal Academy of Music. Principal oboe London orchestras. Band-Master 2nd Regiment of Lifeguards 1849-1856.

Devrient, Eduard Philipp (1801-1877)
German baritone and librettist. Friend of Mendelssohn. Successful opera-singer and theatre reformer. Chief producer and actor Dresden Court Theatre 1844-1846.

Forest, William Charles (1820-1902)
Professional soldier. Promoted Captain 1840. Lt. Gen. 1877.

Gauntlett, Dr Henry John (1805-1876)
Trained as lawyer. Organist and composer. Played organ first performance *Elijah*. Designed organs. Composed many hymn tunes including *Once in Royal David's City*.

Grisi, Guilia (1811-1869)
Italian soprano. Début 1828 Bologna.

Hansom, Joseph Aloyius (1803-1882)
Architect and inventor. Designed Birmingham Town Hall, completed 1833 with his resultant bankruptcy. Registered Patent Safety Cab (No. 6733). Later known as Hansom Cab (1834).

Hahn-Hahn, Ida Marie Luise Gustave Gräfin (1805-1880)
German novelist of the 'Society School'. Married her cousin of same name. Converted to Catholicism. Founded convent at Mainz.

Hawes, Maria Billington (1816-1886)
English contralto. Daughter of William Hawes.

Hill, William and Son
Organ-builders founded 1755 by John Snetzler. Name changed when William Hill became partner 1835. Built organs for York Minster, Ely, Worcester and Manchester cathedrals as well as Birmingham Town Hall.

Hutton, William (1723-1815)
Local historian. Author *History of Birmingham* 1782. Later brought up to date by daughter Catherine.

Jullien, Louis (1812-1860)
French composer and conductor. Played significant role in establishment of the promenade concert. Aimed to attract large audiences by popularising the classics by means of special effects.

Klingemann, Carl (1798-1862)
German Librettist of *Elijah*. Friend of Mendelssohn.

Lind, Jenny (1820-1887)
Known as the 'Swedish Nightingale'. London début *Robert le Diable* 1847. Excelled coloratura roles. Held in high esteem by Mendelssohn.

Liszt, Franz (1820-1886)
World-famous Hungarian composer and pianist. Child prodigy. First piano recital aged nine.

Lockey, Charles (1811-1901)
English tenor. Sang first performance *Elijah*. Appointed Gentleman of Chapel Royal 1848.

Mario, Giovanni Matteo (1810-1883)
Italian tenor. Paris début 1838.

Mendelssohn, Felix Bartholdy (1809-1847)
German-Jewish composer, conductor and organist. Born Frankfurt. Died Leipzig. Child prodigy. Dominated European scene. Composed choral, piano, organ, chamber and orchestral music. Friend of Goethe. Life and works well-documented.

Mitford, Mary Russell (1787-1835)
English novelist. Remembered for *Our Village* a series of sketches of rural life.

Moore, Joseph (1766-1851)
Birmingham benefactor. Friend of Matthew Boulton and later James Watt. Dominated the Birmingham Festival scene for over fifty years.

Moscheles, Ignaz (1794-1870)
Czech composer, pianist and conductor. Co-conductor with Mendelssohn 1846 Festival.

Muntz, George Frederick (1794-1857)
Political reformer and Birmingham M.P. Wealthy industrialist remembered for Muntz Metal and advocacy of Catholic Emancipation.

Neukom, Sigismund Rittervon (1778-1858)
Austrian composer. Studied under Haydn. Lived London and Paris.

Paganini, Nicolo (1782-1840)
Italian virtuosi violinist and composer. First tour at thirteen. Died cancer of larynx.

Pemberton, Charles Reece (1790-1840)
Actor, writer, lecturer. Shylock at Covent Garden 1824 and later at Theatre Royal, Birmingham.

Philips, Henry (1801-1876)
English baritone. Appeared Covent Garden 1824. Appointed principal bass of Ancient Music 1825.

Pountney, William (1820-1903)
Birmingham bass. *Memoirs* relate his experience of Birmingham Festivals from 1846-1903.

Prospère, Jean Guiver (1814-18??)
Ophicleide player. Came to London with the conductor Jullien. Became star performer.

Staudigl, Joseph (1807-1861)
Austrian bass. Active Vienna. Appeared Covent Garden and Her Majesty's Theatre London. Title role in first performance of *Elijah*, Birmingham 1846.

Stimpson, James (1820-1886)
Gifted organist and choir trainer. Chorister Durham Cathedral 1827. Organist in Charge, Carlisle Cathedral 1841-3. Organist Birmingham Town Hall 1843-55. Active Birmingham musical life. Founder of BFCS 1843. Premiered *Concerts Monstres* 1845. Trained BFCS *Elijah* 1846.

White, William (1820-1900)
Quaker counsellor and mayor of Birmingham 1882. Responsible with Joseph Chamberlain and others for slum clearance and the building of Corporation Street.

Wilkes, Mark (dates unknown)
Clerk in mercantile house in Birmingham. Member Canon Street Baptist Church. Later Minister Lady Huntingdon's Chapel Norwich. Author, *Poetical Dream* circa 1774.

Wrottesley, Sir John 2nd Baron (1798-1867)
Equity lawyer. Amateur astronomer. Own observatory. Author, *Catalogue of the Right Ascensions of 1318 Stars*. President Royal Astronomical Society 1854. President Birmingham Triennial Music Festival 1846.

Appendix 3

ELIJAH REVISITED – 13/04/2008

Tonight we are in for a treat. A performance of Mendelssohn's *Elijah*, originally premiered in 1846 by the Maestro in this very building. A building conceived as a magnificent music hall and fitting home for Birmingham's Triennial Festivals, now newly restored with that controversial upper gallery removed, to re-emerge in all its classical splendour.

There are threads of history which run through all this. The Birmingham Festival Choral Society, which is performing tonight, has its roots in the nineteenth century. It was established in 1843, participated in the premiere of *Elijah* and down the years, has remained a vibrant force at the heart of much of Birmingham's musical culture. In Mendelssohn's day it was around two hundred and eighty strong. It comprised seventy nine sopranos, sixty male altos or "bearded altos" as the Maestro called them, sixty tenors and seventy two basses. Not all the singers hailed from around Birmingham. Today, the choir is made up entirely of local talent and is approximately one hundred and thirty strong.

There is an amusing and well authenticated story relating to the original choir which was involved in a strike! It came about because younger members wished, when not taking part, to be permitted to sit among the audience. The older men were already allowed this privilege; so there was a confrontation with the Management- and they walked out, only to return when the issue was resolved. I am sure that such a problem has not arisen today!

BFCS is accompanied tonight by the English Haydn Orchestra under the directorship of Patrick Larley. As the aim is for authenticity, the players will be using period instruments and as musicians know, this can present problems. One of these relates to the magnificent Town Hall organ. In Mendelssohn's day *The Times* described its pipes resembling:

> gigantic rolls of oil cloth (which) rose up from behind its head (touching) the roof like some vast gigantic animal of mysterious form.

Unfortunately, however impressive, this marvellous instrument will not be used tonight. This is because, over the years, it has been rebuilt to accommodate the higher pitch of modern orchestral instruments. Then there is the question of the ophicleide which is now obsolete. But Mendelssohn scored for one, and in 1846, Monsieur Prospère with his "monstre" ophicleide, a brass instrument which resembled an enormous, upturned ice – cream cornet, was a great favourite with the audience and press alike. Today, its role is usually played by the bass tuba; but English Haydn Orchestra are hoping to use an ophicleide in this performance.

Tonight's audience will benefit from greatly improved facilities. In 1846, the ladies were ill-catered for. Original plans for the Town Hall indicate that they were only provided with ONE public convenience! Records show that on that day there were upwards of two thousand people crammed into the building; and because of the numerous encores, it is likely that they would have remained in their seats for anything up to five hours. No more needs to be said.

Thankfully, modern amenities in the Town Hall are ample, including spacious seats in the body of the hall which replace the benches used in 1846. Here Mendelssohn's audience sat jammed together in stifling heat, expectantly awaiting the Maestro's arrival, whose light and slight figure was to step out on to the rostrum at precisely eleven thirty that morning.
Who, says *The Times*:

> Waved his baton to begin... (before) Herr Staudigl... delivered in a voice of thunder the awful predictions of the prophet, Elijah.

So, too, we wait expectantly tonight. We wait for Patrick Larley to make his entrance and for Mark Rowlinson who sings Elijah, again to thrill us with dire predictions.

Audrey Duggan

Appendix 4

PAGES FROM THE 1846 PROGRAMME

BIRMINGHAM MUSICAL FESTIVAL,

IN

AID OF THE FUNDS

OF

THE GENERAL HOSPITAL

AUGUST 25th, 26th, 27th, and 28th,

1846.

BIRMINGHAM:

PRINTED BY JOHN TONKS, HILL-STREET, OPPOSITE THE TOWN HALL.

MDCCCXLVI.

4

PRINCIPAL VOCAL PERFORMERS.

Soprano.

MADAME GRISI, MADAME CARADORI ALLAN.
MISS BASSANO, MISS A. WILLIAMS.

Contralto.

MISS MARIA B. HAWES MISS M. WILLIAMS.

Tenor.

SIGNOR MARIO, MR. BRAHAM,
MR. HOBBS, MR. LOCKEY.

Bass.

HERR STAUDIGL, MR. H. PHILLIPS,
SIGNOR F. LABLACHE, MR. MACHIN.

Leaders.

For the Morning,—MR. T. COOKE, For the Evening,—MR. WILLY.

At the Organ.

DR. GAUNTLETT, and MR. STIMPSON.

Conductors.

DR. F. MENDELSSOHN BARTHOLDY, and MR. MOSCHELES.

Sub-Conductor.

MR. MUNDEN.

Chorus Master.

MR. STIMPSON.

5

THE BAND.

VIOLINS.

Mr. T. Cooke, } Mr. Willy, }	*Leaders, London*
Mr. Watts, *prin. second*	...
Messrs. Blagrove	
Dando	...
Griesbach	...
Thirlwall	...
W. Cramer	...
J. Loder	...
Perry	...
Payton	...
Pigott	...
Anderson	...
E. W. Thomas	...
W. Thomas	...
Hughes	...
Guynemer	...
Watkins	...
Westrop	...
J. B. Calkin	...
Marshall	...
Case	...
Jay	...
W. Blagrove	...
Hope	...
T. Shargool	...
Mellon	...
Eames	...
E. Chipp	...
Travers	...
C. Smith	...
Schikle	...
H. Haywood	*W. Hampton*
Seymour	*Manchester*
Cooper	*Bristol*
Farmer	*Nottingham*
Frobisher	*Halifax*
Clayton	*Warwick*
McEwen	*Coventry*
Flersheim	*Birmingham*
Allwood	...
Start	...

VIOLINS.

Messrs. Beere	*Birmingham*
G. Hayward	...
Hawkes	...
Timmins	...
Jones	...

VIOLAS

Mr. Hill, *Principal*	*London*
Messrs. Kearns	...
Alsept	...
Glanville	...
Lyon	...
Weslake	...
Goffrie	...
J. J. Calkin	...
S. Calkin	...
E Westrop	...
Day	...
Zerbini	...
Tutton	...
Giles	*Hull*
E. Shargool	*Stafford*
Gillins	*Preston*
Wood	*Birmingham*
Grady	...
Heath	...
Adderley	...

VIOLONCELLOS.

Mr. R. Lindley, *prin.*	*London*
Messrs. Lucas	...
Banister	...
Hatton	...
W. Lindley	...
Hancock	...
W. Loder	...
Phillips	...
J. Calkin	...

VIOLONCELLOS.

Messrs. Hausman	*London*
Goodban	...
Guest	...
Pigott	*Dublin*
Reinagle	*Oxford*
Scruton	*Birmingham*
Testar	...

DOUBLE BASSES.

Mr. Howell, *principal*	*London*
Messrs. Casolani	...
Castell	...
Severn	...
Flower	...
Griffiths	...
Pratten	...
Schrœder	...
Moreton, jun.	*Birmingham*
Chattaway	...

FLUTES.

Mr. Ribas, *principal*	*London*
Mr. Card, *prin. second*	...
Messrs Stanier	*Birmingham*
Scriven	...

OBOES.

Mr. G. Cooke, *prin.*	*London*
Messrs. Nicholson	...
Heidlemann	*Birmingham*
Carey	...

CLARIONETTS

Mr. Williams, *prin.*	*London*
Messrs. Lazarus	...
Roxby	*Birmingham*
Pritchard	...

6

HORNS.

Mr. Platt, *principal*	*London*
Messrs. Rae	...
C. Harper	...
H. Probin	*Birmingham*

BASSOONS.

M. Baumann, *prin.*	*London*
Messrs. Godfrey	...
Blyth	*Birmingham*
Dowdie	...

TRUMPETS.

Mr. Harper, *principal*	*London*
Messrs. Irwin	...
Harper, jun.	...
Marson	*Birmingham*

TROMBONES.

Messrs. Smithies	*London*
Cioffi	...
Germann	...

OPHICLEIDES.

Messrs. Ellison	*London*
Thurstan	*Birmingham*

MONSTRE OPHICLEIDE.

M. Prospere	*London*

DRUMS

Mr. Moreton	*Birmingham*

DOUBLE DRUMS.

Mr. Chipp	*London*

THE CHORUS.

SOPRANO.

Miss Ashton	*London*
Aston	*Birmingham*
C. Aston	...
Mrs. Byers	*London*
Miss Byers	...
E. Byers	...
Bourke	...
Mrs. Brenan	...
Miss Boden	...
Miss Rosa Boden	...
Miss Bond	*Birmingham*
Bellamy	...
Bayliss	...
Mrs. Bladder	...
Brookes	...
Miss Barlow	...
E. Barlow	...
M. Barlow	...
Mrs. Catley	...
Cooke	...
Miss Cracknell	...
M. Cracknell	...
Cornet	...
Master Carter	...
Miss Dubois	*London*
Deither	...
L. Deither	...

SOPRANO.

Mrs. Davis	*Birmingham*
Dudley	...
Miss Davis	...
Doody	...
Eades	...
Master Elliott	...
Egginton	...
Miss Freeth	...
Fleet	...
Mrs. Goldsmith	*London*
Miss Harris	...
Mrs. Howse	*Birmingham*
Hobson	...
Miss Harrod	...
Master Humphries	...
Miss Horton	...
Jackson	*London*
A. Jackson	...
Miss Johnson	*Birmingham*
Master Joesbery	...
Miss Johnson	...
Lilley	...
Miss Morris	*London*
Mrs. Mapleson	...
Miss Morley	*Birmingham*
Mrs. Osborne	...
Peck	*London*

SOPRANO

Mrs. Phillips	*Birmingham*
Miss Pursall	...
Mrs. Peace	...
Miss Parry	...
Mrs Poole	...
Miss Parker	...
Master Pittman	...
Miss Reddin	...
Rogers	...
Mrs. Smythson	*London*
Miss Stevens	*Birmingham*
Mrs. Stevens	...
Sadler	...
Smith	...
Master Smith	...
Mrs. Trory	*London*
Miss Tweedie	...
Mrs. Timmins	*Birmingham*
Miss Thistlewood	...
Thorneywork	...
Mrs. Wood	...
Miss Worrall	...
Whitworth	...
Mrs. Walker	...
Miss Whittall	...

7

ALTO.

Mr.	Ashton	*London*
	Adams	*Birmingham*
	Anderson	...
	Allen	...
	Baker, jun.	...
	Baker	...
	Barlow	...
	Blakemore	...
	Banford	...
	J. Benn	...
	Brown	...
	Clouch	...
Master	Cooper	...
Mr.	Duke	...
	Eades	...
	Eades, jun.	...
	Egerton	...
	Forster	*London*
	Field	*Birmingham*
	Freeth	...
	Forman	...
	Fellows	...
	Griffin	*London*
	Genge	...
	Henshaw	*Birmingham*
	Husk	*London*
	Hill	...
	J. T. Hill	...
	Harding	*Birmingham*
	Hutchings	...
	Hall	...
	Humphries	...
	Johnson	*London*
	Jolly	*Birmingham*
	Lomax	*London*
	Lander	*Birmingham*
	Lewis	...
	Miller	*London*
	F. Miller	...
	Mason	*Birmingham*
	Morley	...
	Osborne	...
	Osborne	...
	Parker	...
	Raikes	*London*
	Ridgway	*Birmingham*
	Richards	...

ALTO.

Mr.	Stone	*Birmingham*
	Smith	...
	Stilliard	...
	Simmons	...
	Thornton	...
	Taylor	...
	Walker	*London*
	Waring	*Birmingham*
	E. Waring	...
	Wilmot	...
	Wright	...
	Watkins	...
	Wale	...

TENOR.

Mr.	Ashford	...
	Barlow	...
	V. Betts	...
	Betts	...
	Brooks	...
	Brecknell	...
	Bragg	...
	Carmichael	*London*
	Cooke	*Birmingham*
	E. Cutler	...
	C. Cutler	...
	Cracknell	...
	J Caswell	...
	T. Caswell	...
	Cooper	...
	Deakin	...
	Dudley	...
	Dobbs	...
	Dabbs	...
	Grice	*London*
	Gunter	...
	Hayden	...
	Humphries	*Birmingham*
	Henshaw	...
	Hobson	...
	Heritage	...
	Jones	*London*
	James	*Birmingham*
	Jeff	...
	Langley	...
	Morgan	*London*
	Mitchell	...

TENOR.

Mr.	Marson	*Birmingham*
	Mountford	...
	Peacock	*London*
	Pendleton	*Birmingham*
	Price	*London*
	J. Price	...
	Peck	*Birmingham*
	Poole	...
	Pearsall	...
	Paddy	...
	Pendleton	...
	E. Price	...
	Roberts	...
	Ray	...
	Rayer	...
	Surman	*London*
	Sharp	...
	Smith	*Birmingham*
	Trory	*London*
	Tandy	*Birmingham*
	Taylor	...
	Thomas	...
	Taylor	...
	J. Taylor	...
	Williams	*London*
	Woodward	*Birmingham*
	Walton	...
	Wright	...

BASS.

Mr.	Arrowsmith	*Birmingham*
	Aston	...
	Allen	...
	J. Aston	...
	Beale	*London*
	Bowley	...
	Butler	...
	Barnby	...
	Barwell, sen.	*Birmingham*
	J. Barwell	...
	Barford	...
	Bell	...
	Baker	...
	Bainbridge	...
	Badger	...
	Ball	...
	Bowley	...
	Bullus	...

8

BASS.

Mr.	Brown	*Birmingham*
	Brittain	...
	Collett	*London*
	Carter	*Birmingham*
	Coburn	...
	Davis	*London*
	Doley	*Birmingham*
	Duke	...
	Egginton	...
	Ellioott	...
	Edwards	...
	W. T. Edwards	...
	G. W. Elliott	...
	Frost	*London*
	Feuney	*Birmingham*
	Gough	...
	Green	*London*
	Gosling	*Birmingham*

BASS.

Mr.	Hawker	*London*
	E. Hughes	*Birmingham*
	Hughes	...
	Hehl	*London*
	Hilliley	*Birmingham*
	Joesbery	...
	Kerby	...
	Linyard	...
	Langston	...
	Machain	...
	Morgan	...
	McCarthy	*London*
	Martin	*Birmingham*
	Newton	...
	Owens	...
	Oxford	...
	Parker	...
	Peace	...

BASS.

Mr.	Poole	*Birmingham*
	Prince	...
	Plows	...
	Pountney	...
	Ridgway	...
	Simmonds	*London*
	Smythson	...
	Stevens	*Birmingham*
	Smith	...
	C. Smith	...
	Savage	...
	Sutton	...
	Taylor	...
	Trunnel	...
	Williamson	*London*
	Woolley	*Birmingham*
	Walker	...
	Waddington	...

☞ ***The Author of this English Version of the Oratorio of* Elijah *has endeavoured to render it as nearly in accordance with the scriptural texts as the music to which it is adapted will admit.***

ELIJAH,

A SACRED ORATORIO.

PART FIRST.

PROLOGUE—(Elijah.)

As God the Lord of Israel liveth, before whom I stand, there shall not be dew nor rain these years, but according to my word.—1 *Kings* i, 17.

OVERTURE.

CHORUS—(The People.)

Help, Lord! wilt thou quite destroy us?

The harvest now is over, the summer days are gone, and yet no power cometh to help us! Will, then, the Lord be no more God in Zion?—*Jeremiah* viii, 20.

RECITATIVE CHORUS—(The People.)

The deeps afford no water; and the rivers are exhausted!

The suckling's tongue now cleaveth for thirst to its mouth; the infant children ask for bread, and there is no one breaketh it to feed them.—*Lamentations* iv, 4.

WEDNESDAY MORNING.

Part First.

Prologue—Herr Staudigl, "As God the Lord of Israel liveth."
Overture.
Chorus—"Help, Lord!"
Recitative Chorus—"The deeps afford no water."
{ *Duet*—Madame Caradori Allan and Miss Bassano, "Zion spreadeth her hands."
{ *Chorus*—"Lord, bow thine ear."
Recitative and Air—Mr. Lockey, "Ye people, rend your hearts."
Chorus—"Yet doth the Lord see it not."
Recitative—Miss M. B. Hawes, "Elijah! get thee hence."
Double Quartet—Misses. A. Williams, Bassano, M. Williams, M. B. Hawes, Messrs. Hobbs, Lockey, Phillips, and Machin, "For He shall give His angels charge."
Recitative—Miss M. B. Hawes, "Elijah! now Cherith's brook is dried up."
Air—Madame Caradori Allan, "Help me, man of God."
Recitative—Madame Caradori Allan and Herr Staudigl, "Give me thy son."
Chorus—"Blessed are the men who fear Him."
Recitative—Mr. Hobbs, Herr Staudigl, and Chorus, "As God the Lord of Sabaoth."
Chorus—"Baal, we cry to thee!"
Recitative—Herr Staudigl, "Call him louder, for he is a god!"
Chorus—"Hear our cry, O Baal!"
Recitative—Herr Staudigl, "Call him louder, he heareth not!"
Chorus—"Hear and answer, Baal!"
Recitative and Air—Herr Staudigl, "Draw near, all ye people."
Quartet—Madame Caradori Allan, Miss M. B. Hawes, Mr. Hobbs, and Mr. Phillips, "Regard thy servant's prayer."
Recitative—Herr Staudigl, "O Thou who makest."
Chorus—"The fire descends from heaven."
Recitative—Herr Staudigl, "Take all the priests of Baal."
Air—Herr Staudigl, "Is not His word like a fire?"
Air—Miss M. B. Hawes, "Woe unto them who forsake Him!"
Recitative—Madame Caradori Allan and Herr Staudigl, with Chorus, "O Lord, Thou hast overthrown Thine enemies."
Recitative—Herr Staudigl and Chorus, "Thanks be to God for all His mercies."
Chorus—"Thanks be to God! He laveth the thirsty land."

AN INTERVAL OF TWENTY MINUTES.

WEDNESDAY MORNING.

Part Second.

Recitative—Mr. Hobbs, "Elijah is come already."
Air—Madame Caradori Allan, "Hear ye, Israel!"
Chorus—"Be not afraid."
Recitative—Herr Staudigl, "Yet, Ahab, thou hast not."
Recitative—Miss M. B. Hawes, "Dost thou now govern?"
Chorus—"Do unto him as he hath done."
Recitative and Air—Herr Staudigl, "Though stricken, they have not grieved."
Recitative—Mr. Hobbs, "Under a juniper tree."
Duet—The Misses Williams, "Lift thine eyes."
Chorus—"He, watching over Israel."
Recitative—Miss M. B. Hawes and Herr Staudigl, "Arise, Elijah."
Air—Miss M. B. Hawes, "O rest in the Lord."
Chorus—"He that shall endure to the end."
Recitative—Madame Caradori Allan and Herr Staudigl, "Hear me speedily, O Lord."
Chorus—"And behold the Lord passed by."
Quartet with Chorus—Madame Caradori Allan, Misses Bassano, M. Williams, and M. B. Hawes, "Holy, holy!"
Recitative—Herr Staudigl, "O Lord, I have heard of Thee!"
Air—Herr Staudigl, "For the mountains shall depart."
Chorus—"Then did Elijah the prophet."
Air—Mr. Lockey, "Then shall the righteous shine forth."
Recitative—Miss M. Williams, "Elijah walked with God."
Recitative—Miss Bassano, "Behold! the Lord will send."
Chorus—"But thus saith the Lord."
Quartet—Madame Caradori Allan, Miss Bassano, Messrs. Hobbs and Phillips, "O! every one that thirsteth."
Chorus—"Unto Him that is abundantly able."

AN INTERVAL OF FIVE MINUTES.

Part Third.

Aria—Signor Mario, "A te fra tante affanni" . . . *Davide Penitente* Mozart.
Recitative and Aria—Madame Grisi, "Ah parlate" . *Il sacrificio d' Abramo* Cimaroso.
Coronation Anthem—"The king shall rejoice" . . . . Handel.

Under the Especial Patronage of

HER MOST GRACIOUS MAJESTY, THE QUEEN.

HER MAJESTY THE QUEEN DOWAGER.

HIS ROYAL HIGHNESS THE PRINCE ALBERT.

HIS ROYAL HIGHNESS THE DUKE OF CAMBRIDGE.

HER ROYAL HIGHNESS THE DUCHESS OF KENT.

President.

THE RIGHT HONOURABLE THE LORD WROTTESLEY.

Vice-Presidents.

The LORD ARCHBISHOP OF YORK
The DUKE OF MARLBOROUGH
The DUKE OF SUTHERLAND, K.G.
The EARL OF SHREWSBURY
The EARL OF DENBIGH
The EARL OF DARTMOUTH
The EARL OF AYLESFORD
The EARL BROOKE & WARWICK, K.T.
The EARL OF CLARENDON
The EARL TALBOT, K.G.
The EARL OF CRAVEN
The EARL OF HARROWBY
The EARL OF BRADFORD
The EARL BEAUCHAMP
The EARL HOWE
The VISCOUNT LIFFORD
The VISCOUNT LEWISHAM
The LORD GUERNSEY
The LORD BROOKE, M.P.
The VISCOUNT INGESTRIE, M.P.
The VISCOUNT SANDON, M.P.
The VISCOUNT NEWPORT, M.P.
The VISCOUNT CURZON
The LORD BISHOP OF WORCESTER
The LORD BISHOP OF LICHFIELD
The LORD WILLOUGHBY DE BROKE
The LORD DORMER
The LORD WARD
The LORD LYTTLETON
The LORD CALTHORPE
The LORD SANDYS
The LORD HATHERTON
The LORD LEIGH
CHARLES THOMAS WARDE, Esq., High Sheriff of Warwickshire

The RT. HON. SIR R. PEEL, Bart, M.P.
The RT. HON. WILLIAM YATES PEEL
The HON. AND VERY REV. THE DEAN OF LICHFIELD
The HON. ROBERT HENRY CLIVE, M.P.
The HON. COL. GEORGE ANSON, M.P.
SIR GRAY SKIPWITH, Bart
SIR J. R. CAVE BROWNE CAVE, Bart
SIR FRANCIS LAWLEY, Bart
SIR R. GEORGE THROCKMORTON, Bart
SIR THEOPHILUS BIDDULPH, Bart
SIR T. E. WINNINGTON, Bart, M.P.
SIR EDMUND CRADDOCK HARTOPP, Bart
SIR E. D. SCOTT, Bart
SIR GEORGE PHILLIPS, Bart
SIR F. L. HOLYOAKE GOODRICKE, Bart
SIR JOHN F. PACKINGTON, Bart
LIEUT. GEN. SIR A. F. BARNARD, G.C.B.
The VERY REV. the DEAN OF WORCESTER
COL. THORN, C.B., K.H.
WILLIAM STRATFORD DUGDALE, Esq. M.P.
CHARLES NEWDIGATE NEWDEGATE, Esq., M.P.
EVELYN JOHN SHIRLEY, Esq., M.P.
JAMES ARTHUR TAYLOR, Esq., M.P.
CHARLES BOWYER ADDERLEY, Esq., M.P.
RICHARD SPOONER, Esq., M.P.
GEORGE FREDERICK MUNTZ, Esq., M.P.
EDWARD BOLTON KING, Esq.
CAPTAIN INGE
JOHN HODGETTS HODGETTS FOLEY, Esq.
JAMES TAYLOR, Esq.
HENRY SMITH, Esq., Mayor of Birmingham
JOSEPH FREDERICK LEDSAM, Esq.